Kamishibai
Story Theater

Kamishibai Story Theater

The Art of Picture Telling

Dianne de Las Casas

Illustrated by Philip Chow

Teacher Ideas Press, an imprint of Libraries Unlimited
Westport, Connecticut ▪ London

Library of Congress Cataloging-in-Publication Data

De las Casas, Dianne.
   Kamishibai story theater : the art of picture telling / Dianne de
las Casas ; illustrated by Philip Chow.
     p. cm.
  Includes bibliographical references and index.
  ISBN 1-59158-404-3 (pbk. : alk. paper)
  1. Kamishibai. 2. Kamishibai—History and criticism.
3. Kamishibai in education. I. Title.
  PN1979.K3D4 2006
  372.66—dc22   2006023745

British Library Cataloguing in Publication Data is available.

Library of Congress Catalog Card Number: 2006023745
ISBN: 1-59158-404-3

First published in 2006

Libraries Unlimited/Teacher Ideas Press, 88 Post Road West, Westport, CT 06881
A Member of the Greenwood Publishing Group, Inc.
www.lu.com

Printed in the United States of America

The paper used in this book complies with the
Permanent Paper Standard issued by the National
Information Standards Organization (Z39.48–1984).

10 9 8 7 6 5 4 3 2 1

Contents

Folktales from Asia

Introduction

My work in storytelling has led me to become a teaching artist in the classroom. In my school residencies, I work for an extended period with the students, teaching them storytelling techniques. The residency often culminates in a student performance of the "Story Fest." Much of my residency work focuses on Story Theater. In my method of Story Theater, the entire class has the opportunity to participate.

As a child, I grew up listening to stories about Japan. My father, who was in the U.S. Navy, lived in Japan for a few years. He had an obvious love for the country, its people, and its culture. Through my father's tales, I fell in love with Japan as well.

A few years ago, I attended an arts in education institute in Louisiana and was introduced to Kamishibai by June Labyzon, an instructor who spent time in Japan and learned the art of Kamishibai. I fell in love again; this time with Kamishibai. It was storytelling, drama, and visual arts combined. And it was from Japan! I knew I had to use Kamishibai in the classroom.

I researched Kamishibai and learned as much as I could. When my friend school librarian Ellen Miller asked me to do a residency for her school's third-, fourth-, and fifth-grade classes, I said excitedly, "I have a new idea." Using Kamishibai techniques, I developed a method of Kamishibai Story Theater that involves the entire classroom of students in the telling of one story. It is creative, fun, and the students enjoyed the process.

This book outlines three methods of Kamishibai: classroom kamishibai, in which the whole class shares in the telling a single tale; individual student Kamishibai, in which individual students perform traditional Kamishibai; and student-created Kamishibai, in which the students create and perform their original stories.

Included are twenty-five stories from Asia. Although the largest number of stories are from Japan, I chose stories from other parts of Asia that I thought worked well not only in telling, but also in illustration. There are other Asian countries with a tradition of picture telling, although Kamishibai is unique to Japan. Picture telling is thought to have originated in China; however, Burma, Laos, Thailand, and Vietnam have a tradition of story cloths.

I want to acknowledge my artist, Philip Chow, who is from China. His elegant original drawings in black and white capture the spirit of Kamishibai. Thank you, Phil.

I hope you, too, will fall in love with Kamishibai. Clap! Clap! Let the stories begin!
Mukashimukashi …
Once Upon a Time …

Background of Kamishibai

In the Japanese language, *Kamishibai* (kah-MEE-shee-bye) means "paper drama." Kamishibai was a popular form of street storytelling from the late 1920s until the early 1950s. The Kamishibai man was an itinerant storyteller who traveled from village to village or neighborhood to neighborhood by bicycle. His main occupation was selling candy. To entice children to buy candy, he entertained them with stories.

To announce his arrival, he loudly clapped together two pieces of wood called *hyoshigi* (hee-yo-SHEE-gee). When the children heard the clapping, they came running much as today's children do when they hear the sound of the ice cream truck. Children who purchased candy were privileged with a position in the front. Those who did not buy candy were still able to stand behind paying customers and listen to the stories.

The Kamishibai man inserted large, often self-created, illustrated story cards into a wooden stage strapped to the back of the bicycle. He began by saying, "Mukashimukashi," meaning "Once Upon a Time...." He dramatized the stories with great flair, with each scene accompanied by the illustrated story cards. He told the stories in serial fashion, and when he came to an exciting moment in the story, he stopped, creating a cliffhanger. This technique created anticipation for his next visit.

Kamishibai flourished in Japan at a time during great economic depression during and after World War II. Kamishibai was portable, and it became the poor man's theater, entertaining adults as well as children. The art form allowed those who had lost their jobs due to the war the ability to earn a meager living as a Kamishibai man. Unfortunately, with the advent of television came the demise of Kamishibai. Adults and children became more interested in the excitement of the moving pictures and sound that television offered.

Recently, Kamishibai has enjoyed a renaissance because schoolteachers and librarians have revived this Japanese art of picture telling for the benefit of their children.

The Kamishibai Story Theater Process

Introduction to Story Theater

Story Theater is the narration of events through dramatic performance. In Story Theater, the storyteller performs or dramatizes the stories through vocal inflections, facial expressions, and body movement.

There is no one right way to tell a story. Every storytelling style has value. With that in mind, storytelling and Kamishibai Story Theater is a perfect way for students with varied learning styles to communicate their creativity.

Before I begin explaining how Kamishibai works and how to implement it in the classroom, I would like to share some important techniques that will help your students acclimate to the atmosphere of Story Theater.

Establishing an Environment of Trust

To "break the ice" so that the students can get to know me better, I begin with a self-created Kamishibai story. The act of storytelling is an intimate art and allows the students to get to know me, thus allowing them to trust me. You can retell a traditional Japanese or Asian tale, or even recount an important event in your life history through Kamishibai.

In Story Theater, trust is very important. Through the act of dramatization, storytellers often expose themselves and their emotions in a way never seen before. It is the same for the students. Some of the students may have never had the opportunity to role-play or act out a part and may feel uncomfortable doing so in front of their peers. In addition, students who are not accustomed to sharing their artwork in a community setting may also feel self-conscious.

To establish the environment of trust, I introduce "The Classroom Contract," a contract for grades 3 and up that enforces respect and prevents teasing. It is read orally and at the end of each statement, the students say, "I agree." It helps set expectations and guidelines for the duration of my work with the students.

Classroom Contract

The Number One Rule is RESPECT

- RESPECT FELLOW CLASSMATES—I will respect my classmates at all times. I will not laugh at them, make fun of them, or make them feel bad.

2

- RESPECT TEACHER—I will respect [teacher's name] by listening to her and following directions. Failure to do so will result in a behavior report [or other means of discipline suited to your school's environment].

- RESPECT OTHER PEOPLE'S PROPERTY—I will respect other people's property including my fellow classmates and my teacher(s). I will take care of borrowed items and put them back where they belong.

Although I find that an oral contract suffices, you can provide a signature line and have each student sign the contract. If the class becomes unruly, I simply pull out the Classroom Contract and issue a gentle reminder.

Introducing Kamishibai to Your Students

Kamishibai Story Theater involves not only the dramatization of stories but a visual art element as well. It is a great way to incorporate language arts, social studies, and visual arts simultaneously into a lesson. Students strengthen their sequencing and presentation skills and learn about another culture. With self-created Kamishibai, students also strengthen their writing skills. The teacher or students can create Kamishibai cards inexpensively on large poster board. Introduce your class to the concept of Kamishibai by telling them the history of the art form. A good way to do this is with Caldecott-Winning author and illustrator Allen Say's book, *Kamishibai Man*.

A student-illustrated Kamishibai card for "Nida and the Wishing Coconut"

Kamishibai cards are larger than picture books, making the illustrations easier for the entire class to view. There are typically twelve Kamishibai cards in a modern Kamishibai set. The cards are viewed in sequential order, with the text for the front card printed on the back of the last card. When the teller has finished recounting each scene, the card in front is moved to the back. This continues until the story ends. There is no break in the telling of the story. The front and back of the cards are numbered in sequential order to aid the Kamishibai teller in keeping the story sequence correct.

To make telling easier, the cards can rest on a table in front of the teller, a wooden Kamishibai stage can be used, or a tabletop easel can be employed. The teller can also hold the Kamishibai cards in her lap and sit on a chair as the rest of the class sits on the floor. When I create my own Kamishibai cards, I create five story cards, illustrating the most vital scenes of the story. I place the cards on a tabletop easel and sit in a chair next to the table. The Kamishibai cards should be easy to access and change, so that the flow of the storytelling is not interrupted.

Begin with creating the story cards. Once you write your story (or use a traditional Japanese or Asian folktale), choose which scenes you would like to illustrate. You can use as few as five cards or as many as you like. If you are not comfortable retelling the story without prompts, cut the story into manageable sections and glue them to the back of the story cards. Remember to place the text for the first card on the back of the last card. The text for the second card is placed on the back of the first card. The text of the third card is placed on the back of the second card and so forth. The example of your self-created Kamishibai will inspire the students to create their own.

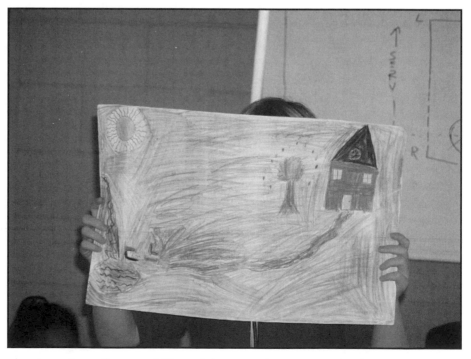

A student-illustrated Kamishibai card for "The Man in the Moon"

Classroom Kamishibai

There are many ways to use Kamishibai in the classroom. This method allows the whole class to present a story together and is a good way to introduce Kamishibai when you don't have a lot of time. Each student will need poster board, scissors, glue, and drawing supplies (crayons, markers, or colored pencils). The poster boards should be cut to the same size for consistency when the story is presented. Modern Kamishibai sets are approximately 11 x 15 inches. For my students, I ordered large poster board from a local art supply store and took it to a printer to be cut in half. The pieces measured approximately 14 x 22 inches. The larger cards allowed the students to create visually stunning illustrations that a large audience had no difficulty viewing.

Select a story and tell or read the story out loud to the class so that they can familiarize themselves with the story. Ask them to visualize the scenes of the story. Each student will be illustrating a scene of the story.

Make a photocopy of your selected story or create your own and print it. Count the number of students in your class. Use a pencil to draw lines dividing the story into that many sections. For example, if you have twenty-five students, the story should be divided into twenty-five sections. Number each of the sections and then cut the story apart. Each student should have a few lines each. It's a good idea to keep a master copy of the story with each student's name written beside his or her lines.

The students will then glue the lines of the story to the poster board. It is helpful to number the Kamishibai cards on back with large numbers so that you can easily track the story's sequence. In the upper left corner on the backside of the poster board, have the students write their names, their teacher's name, and their grade. The title of the story should be written above their story lines. I use a mock poster board to demonstrate. One side has the story lines glued in the middle of the poster board with the title written above it. The student's name, teacher, and grade are printed in the upper left corner of the poster board. The other side has a drawing illustrating the lines of the story. It is laminated for protection and hung at the front of the class so that the students can follow it as an example.

Once the back of the poster board has been completed, have the students turn their poster boards over and illustrate the blank side. Each student will have a different scene to illustrate. Some of your students may feel apprehensive about their artistic abilities. Assure them that you are looking for the flavor of the story and that there is no wrong way to create art. Remind them to create large illustrations so that when they are presenting their part of the story, the rest of the audience will be able to see the pictures. I encourage the students to fill the entire space with color, which gives the Kamishibai cards a vibrant look and makes the presentation vivid.

Keep the Kamishibai cards in the classroom while they are working on them. This eliminates the possibility of the cards being lost or forgotten at home. If your school has an art teacher, the Kamishibai project would be a good opportunity for a collaborative effort between you and that teacher.

Once the Kamishibai cards are completed, the students can begin rehearsing their story. Although they can read their lines, I encourage students to tell their part of the story, which does not mean memorizing their lines. What they tell does not have to match the lines of the story exactly as long as they are conveying what is in their scene. It typically takes four class periods for the process. The first class period is spent with the teacher telling the story, dividing up the story, passing the story lines out, and working on the Kamishibai cards. The second period is spent completing the illustrations. The third period is spent rehearsing the Kamishibai presentation. The fourth period is spent presenting the Kamishibai story. Tips for coaching and creating a grade-level Kamishibai Story Fest are included later in the book.

Individual Student Kamishibai

In this method, students present their own Kamishibai tale in the traditional way. Each student is provided with a Japanese or other Asian folktale. Each student will need poster board, scissors, glue, and drawing supplies (crayons, markers, or colored pencils). As with the method described in the previous section, the poster boards should be cut to the same size. The boards should be a manageable size for the students to handle and be stiff enough so that they do not bend when students hold them.

For elementary students, five to six cards per student works well. It allows students to convey the story without overwhelming them with too many illustrations. Allow the students to divide their own stories for illustration. In this way, they choose which scenes they will illustrate, and it helps them sequence their story.

It may help to have the students create a storyboard outline before they begin cutting apart their story and creating the illustrations. Ask the students to visualize the story and remember the pictures they see. What parts of the story are important? Is there an exciting moment in the story that the listeners must experience? On a separate sheet of paper, have them write down what they think the important scenes are. If there are more than five or six, ask them to choose the most vital scenes. These are the scenes they will illustrate.

A student-illustrated Kamishibai card for "The Cowherd and the Weaving Maiden"

Mount the story on the back of the Kamishibai boards and then number the boards. Remember, the text for the front card is mounted on the back of the last card. The text for the second card is mounted on the back of the first card. This can be confusing for the students, so it helps to have a ready-made set of Kamishibai cards to demonstrate.

Once the Kamishibai boards are illustrated, they will need to be stored. Jumbo envelopes can be purchased online or at an office supply store. Alternatively, students can create their own envelopes using butcher paper or larger poster board for a sturdier envelope. Have the students illustrate and decorate their Kamishibai envelopes with art from the story and the story's title. This will also aid in matching the cards to the envelopes when the cards need to be stored.

When the students present their Kamishibai stories, encourage them to hold their boards at chest level, not in front of their faces. Some students will tend to want to hide behind their Kamishibai cards. Explain that their facial expressions are as important to the story as the illustrations and that holding the cards in front of their faces will muffle their voices, making it difficult for the audience to hear them. Encourage the students to tell their stories rather than read them. If you decide to have your students read the stories, demonstrate how to read their cards without covering their faces or looking down the entire time.

It is such a joy to see students presenting Kamishibai. When they are finished with their presentations, praise their success.

Student-Created Kamishibai

In this method of Kamishibai, students create their own stories that they turn into Kamishibai tales. In student-created Kamishibai, the 6 + 1 traits of writing are naturally addressed:

1. *Idea development*—Students develop the ideas and theme of the story.

2. *Organization*—Students must tell things in order and sequence the events of the story so that the story has a beginning, a middle, and an end.

3. *Voice*—When students create their own tales, their inner writing voice emerges. It is the voice of the story crafter that affects the story reader or listener.

4. *Conventions*—Students make use of a title, spelling, grammar and usage, paragraphing, capitalization, and punctuation.

5. *Sentence fluency*—Because Kamishibai is heavy on sequencing, sentences must make sense for the story to flow properly.

6. *Word choice*—Students make use of nouns, verbs, and adjectives. Because of the folktale nature of Kamishibai, stories tend to be rich in colorful language.

7. *Presentation*—The rhythm and flow of the language comes to life when the Kamishibai tale is shared aloud.

Have the students brainstorm story ideas. Ask them the following questions:

- What do they want to write about?

- Who are the characters in the story?

- What is the plot of the story?

- Where does the story take place?

- What is the conflict in the story?

The Kamishibai stories should have some parameters to guide the students as they are creating their tales. Here a few suggestions:

- Write a story in a folktale style. The use of magic, talking animals, and talking objects is encouraged.

- Stories should have at least two characters, not including the narrator.

- Dialogue must be used between characters.

- The story must have a conflict, a problem that has to be solved by the story's end.

- The story should be no longer than two handwritten, single-spaced, lined pages or three double-spaced, typed pages.

If students are having trouble creating story ideas, provide them with story starters. Here are some sample starters:

There was once an old man. One day, when he was walking to the village, he saw a _____ in the middle of the road. It began talking and said _____.

The earth shook and the sky blackened. When [name of character] peeked out from behind the bushes, he saw _____.

[Name of character] was a poor girl. She had nothing but the clothes on her back. One day, as she sweeping, she saw a mouse. The mouse said _____.

[Name of character] was afraid of goblins. His father told him that if he went into the forest alone, he might be captured. One day, he saw a huge _____.

Rabbit threw a party at a time when the all the animals were friends. But when _____ stole the _____ from _____, everything changed.

To encourage students to create their own story prompts, have them ask themselves, "What if?" For example, "What if pigs could fly?" The answer to the "what if?" question is the story.

Once the students have written their stories, they must select which scenes to illustrate. After selecting the scenes, have the students mount the sequenced story to the back of the poster board as previously discussed. Students will then illustrate their stories and number the Kamishibai cards on the front and back. To complete the project, students can create special envelopes for the Kamishibai cards.

Coaching

Praise and an atmosphere of mutual respect are important for success for both you and your students. Here are some tips for successful coaching:

- Give suggestions rather than telling them how to perform their part. For example, instead of "Amanda, say it like this," try "Amanda, what do you think your character would sound like if he were angry?"

- When praising students, praise specific examples. "Amanda, I like the way you used your body as well as your voice to portray the bear." This will bolster the student's confidence in her abilities.

- If a student is having trouble with her part, speak to her in private. If the student refuses to perform in front of her peers, respect her wishes. Forcing a student to perform when she is not ready can have severe psychological repercussions. If the part must be reassigned, do so without fanfare.

- Sometimes, students may have trouble remembering the story. A quick glance at the illustration can serve as a reminder. If the student still has trouble remembering his lines, offer quiet story prompts. Sometimes signals or hand motions can jog a student's memory.

I have had students with behavioral difficulties absolutely shine in performance. The Kamishibai Story Theater process allows students creative success.

A student-illustrated Kamishibai card for "The Girl Who Used Her Wits"

Rehearsals

Rehearsals allow the students to work through their fears and perfect their presentations. For many students, stage fright or lack of self-confidence is the biggest inhibitor to performance success. Often they are afraid of "messing up" in front of their peers. Assure them that you will help them with reminder lines and prompts.

The other inhibitor to performance success is inadequate preparation. When the students know exactly what to expect, they are more confident in their roles. Some elements to practice:

- Story openings and closings

- Students' positioning on the stage

- Holding the Kamishibai cards correctly

- Entrances and exits

- Microphone usage

Talk openly with the students about ways to counteract stage fright including:

- Taking deep, relaxing breaths

- Warming up with exercises to get the blood moving

- Visualizing the story and working through any mistakes

- Pausing for a moment to collect their thoughts if they blank out

A student-illustrated Kamishibai card for "The Cowherd and the Weaving Maiden"

If you are performing a classroom Kamishibai, it is helpful to have the students stay in line formation in order of the story. They can all be seated but while one teller is at the microphone, the next storyteller stands and gets ready to walk to the microphone. After the teller is finished with his part, he returns to the end of the line.

Work with the students as often as possible, allowing them to tweak their performance and to tighten their timing as a group. Be sure to have your copy of the story handy in the event a Kamishibai card is missing. You may also want to designate "pinch hitters," storytellers who can fill in if someone is absent on the day of the performance.

Presentation Tips—Dramatizing the Stories

When working with the storytellers, encourage them to enunciate their parts clearly and give the characters different voices. Voice inflection and tone are important to the storyteller's performance. Even without great movement, the storyteller can convey drama and emotion in the story with effective use of the voice and facial expressions.

Management and Organization Tips

If you are a drama teacher working with several classes, you may find it helpful to create a binder with tabbed sections for each grade. The tabs organize the Kamishibai stories you are using for each grade. Here are some tips for organizing your binder:

- Sheet protectors help preserve your copies of the Kamishibai stories.

- When you are assigning story lines, write each student's first and last name next to his lines on your copy of the story. Also write the teacher's name and grade at the top of your copy of the story.

- Make personal notes in the margin of your script(s) and keep them in the sheet protectors of your binder.

- Keep extra copies of stories in a folder in your binder for the inevitable moment a Kamishibai card goes missing.

Coordinating a Kamishibai Story Fest

Although the Kamishibai stories are great for in-class use, creating a grade-wide or school-wide Story Fest allows the student storytellers to share their efforts with an appreciative audience. Grade-wide Kamishibai Story Fests, where each class performs for their peers, develop an atmosphere of respect and support because each student performs during the Fest.

Another option is to have the class perform for lower grades. The younger students admire the older students, and the older students come away with a sense of accomplishment.

Still another alternative is to perform a Family Night Kamishibai Story Fest, where parents, grandparents, and other family members are invited. In this scenario, students stand proudly before their families in anticipation of their performance.

Once you have decided on your Kamishibai Story Fest, you will need to work out these details:

- *Location of performance*—Wherever you perform—cafeteria, gym, library, or auditorium—be sure to let the people in charge of that space know ahead of time. They will appreciate the advance notice and can help with preparation.

- *Schedule*—Coordinate scheduling with everyone involved, including other teachers, administration, staff, and parents.

- *Parents*—If parents are invited, send notes home. Creating a colorful invitation sets the tone for a festive mood. Asian-themed paper makes a terrific invitation.

- *Dress*—If the students desire, encourage them to dress up in Asian attire befitting the story.

- *Space*—Be sure that the space is set up for the performance well in advance.

- *Announcements*—Write up a blurb and give it to the morning announcer to remind students and publicize the event.

Kamishibai Story Theater is an exciting form of performance. It works well in classroom settings as well as for larger audiences. Students have the opportunity to shine. Following their performance, reward the students' work by hosting a reception in their honor or passing out award stickers or certificates. A treat of Japanese rice candy would also make a nice surprise. Of course, the most rewarding part of Kamishibai is the process itself. Seeing students performing with their beautiful artwork is a fantastic experience. You can be proud of the fact that you and your class have worked in the line of an age-old tradition of Japanese picture telling, keeping Kamishibai alive and well. *Oshimai.*

The End

Folktales from Asia

The Battle Between Wind and Rain

Philippines

Above the earth, high in the sky, Thunder, Lightning, and Rain were resting in the clouds. Restless Wind danced between them, blowing this way and that way. He said, "Let's make a storm."

Thunder replied, "We just made a fierce storm yesterday. We now need to rest."

Lightning agreed and said, "Yes, it is time to relax."

"But I'm bored," whined the wind. He whirled around the clouds, making them skitter across the sky.

"I am resting, and I wish you would stop that," said Rain irritably. "We are trying to sleep."

Wind laughed. "If you want me to stop, make me. I bet you can't because I am stronger than you!"

Rain answered, "Wild Wind, why don't you ever stay still?"

Wind roared, "I am Wind, the mightiest of all the elements."

Rain said, "Okay, you are the mightiest. Now, may I nap?" Rain closed her eyes.

As soon as she did, Wind blew an icy gust upon her. Rain shivered. Wind said, "Let's play a game. We will see who among us is the mightiest."

Annoyed, Rain said, "Fine. I will play your game. But if I defeat you, you must promise to flee from me."

Wind cried out, "Agreed! But if I defeat you, you must promise never to shed your tears upon the earth again."

Although Rain knew it was a risky bet, she promised. Wind and Rain hovered close above the earth. They saw a monkey climbing the branches of a bamboo tree. Rain said, "Here's the contest. The one who is able to make monkey leave the tree wins."

Wind laughed. "That is easy enough. Wind will win!" Wind drew in a big breath and began blowing. Rain knew that the bamboo would bend in the wind. She hoped that the monkey would hang on.

As wind continued to whip and whirl, the bamboo tree swayed back and forth until it nearly touched the ground. The monkey fiercely hung on to the tree and would not leave.

Rain cried out, "Now it is my turn." The clouds darkened and Rain drizzled. Warm and steady, the rain showered upon the monkey. Still, he held on to the bamboo tree.

"You can't do it!" cried Wind. "The monkey will not let go. No one wins!"

Rain answered, "I am not done." With full force, the sky opened and the water poured down. Huge drops pounded the monkey. Finally, he scampered out of the tree to find cover.

Rain smiled. "I did it! I won!"

Wind whined and wailed. Then he whirled away without a word. He had to keep his promise to Rain and flee whenever she was near.

To this day, when a strong wind rages upon the earth, the people pray for rain because they know that when she comes, the winds will die down. And that is the tale of the battle between Wind and Rain.

The Boy Who Drew Cats

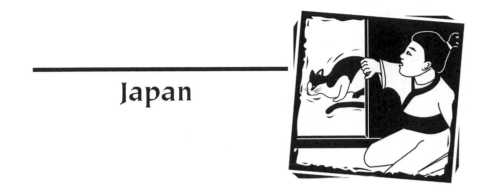

Japan

A long time ago in Japan, there lived a poor farmer and his wife. They had a large family and could barely afford to feed them all. Their youngest son was weak and small, and although he was clever, he was not fit for work.

But he had an unusual gift for drawing cats. He spent all of his time drawing cats!

Big cats, small cats, short cats, tall cats.

Here cats, there cats. Everywhere, cats!

Cats, cats, cats. He drew cats, cats, cats.

His father said, "Son, since you cannot help out on our farm, your mother and I must send you away. You will go to the village temple and study to become a priest."

So the boy was taken to the temple to study the priesthood. An old priest became his teacher, and the boy learned quickly. But at night, when he needed to spend his time studying, he did not. He spent all of his time drawing cats. On the walls and in the halls, on paper and mats, the boy drew cats!

Big cats, small cats, short cats, tall cats.

Here cats, there cats. Everywhere, cats!

Cats, cats, cats. He drew cats, cats, cats.

Although the priest loved the boy dearly, he could not stop him from drawing cats. The old priest called the boy over and said, "Son, since you are unable to study the priesthood, I must send you away. But here is some advice. If you see large places, avoid them all. You must take heed and stick to small."

The boy packed his bundle of clothes and left the temple. He was sad, but he knew the priest was right. He had the heart of an artist, not a priest. He walked for some time and day became night.

The boy began to shiver from the cold and he knew he needed to find shelter. In the distance, he saw a temple. When he knocked on the door, he found it was empty.

He went inside and looked around, "Look at these beautiful floors and those lovely walls!" His heart jumped with joy as he sat down and pulled out his paint and brushes.

He spent all night drawing cats.

Big cats, small cats, short cats, tall cats.

Here cats, there cats. Everywhere, cats!

Cats, cats, cats. He drew cats, cats, cats.

When he was finished, he looked around and was pleased with his work. He was tired and needed to sleep. As he searched the big room for a place to sleep, he remembered the old priest's words. "If you see large places, avoid them all. You must take heed and stick to small."

So the boy found a small cabinet with a sliding door and climbed inside. He started to doze off when he heard strange noises. Hissing and howling. Grunting and growling. The boy was frightened, and he stayed in the small cabinet.

When morning's light came, the sounds stopped. Carefully sliding the door open, the boy stepped out of the cabinet. He looked around. He saw his cats on the floors and on the walls, but they were all in different places and in different positions!

It was then that he saw something lying in the middle of the floor. It was a huge goblin rat. The boy knew immediately that his cats had come to life during the night and saved his life. The boy bowed and said, "Thank you, honorable cats!"

From that time forward, the boy with the heart of an artist drew to his heart's content. And, of course, he spent all of his time drawing cats!

Big cats, small cats, short cats, tall cats.

Here cats, there cats. Everywhere, cats!

Cats, cats, cats. He drew cats, cats, cats.

He became a famous artist known all over Japan for his beautiful drawings of . . . cats!

The Boy Who Wanted a Drum

India

Many years ago, there lived a poor woman and her son. Her son was hardworking and never complained about his ragged clothes and worn shoes. The woman wanted to give her son a special gift. She asked him, "I am going to the market to sell our grain. Is there anything you want from the market?"

The boy had always wished for a drum. He could feel the beat of the drum deep inside his heart. "Mother, I would like a drum," he replied.

The boy's mother went to market and sold her grain. She did not have enough money to buy him a drum, but she didn't want to come home empty-handed. On the way home, she found a sturdy stick. She picked it up and said, "I will give this to my son."

When she handed the stick to her son, he smiled and said, "Thank you, mama." He went outside to play and saw an old woman trying to light her *chulha,* her woodstove. The fire would not start. Big billows of smoke stung her eyes and made her cry.

The boy asked gently, "What is the matter?"

The old woman answered, "I cannot light my fire."

The boy replied, "I have a sturdy stick. You can have it. You need it more than I."

The old woman was delighted. She took the stick and lit her fire. To thank the boy, the old woman gave him a *chapatti*, a round, flat piece of bread.

The boy walked on until he came upon a mother and her crying child.

The boy asked gently, "What is the matter?"

The mother answered, "My child is hungry, and I have nothing to feed him."

The boy replied, "I have a *chapatti*. You can have it. You need it more than I."

The mother, who was the potter's wife, was delighted. She took the bread and fed it to her hungry child. To thank the boy, she gave him a large pot.

The boy walked on until he came upon a couple arguing.

The boy asked gently, "What is the matter?"

The man, a washerman, answered, "The pot I use to wash clothes in is broken. I cannot boil my clothes clean."

The boy replied, "I have a large pot. You can have it. You need it more than I."

The washerman and his wife were delighted. They took the pot and put their clothes inside. To thank the boy, they gave him a warm coat.

The boy walked on until he came to a bridge. There, he saw a man shivering in the cold without even a shirt to cover him.

The boy asked gently, "What is the matter?"

The man answered, "I was attacked by robbers. They stole everything, including my shirt."

The boy replied, "I have a warm coat. You can have it. You need it more than I."

The man was delighted. He put the coat on and it fit perfectly. To thank the boy, he gave him a strong horse that the robbers left behind.

The boy walked on with his horse until he ran into a wedding party with musicians, the bridegroom, and his family. They were sitting under a tree with long faces.

"The boy asked gently, "What is the matter?"

The bridegroom said, "We need a horse for our wedding procession. The man who was supposed to bring us a horse is not here! What shall we do? I will be late for my own wedding!"

The boy replied, "I have a strong horse. You can have it. You need it more than I."

The bridegroom was delighted. "You have saved the day! Let me repay your kindness with a gift." He spoke to one of the musicians and then handed the boy a drum.

The boy was delighted! "I have always wanted a drum. I can feel the drum beat inside my heart. Thank you!"

They celebrated their good fortune with music. The boy waved to the bridegroom as he rode away on his strong horse. Then he ran all the way home.

"Mama, mama," he shouted. Look at my new drum!" He told her his story and then played her the song from deep inside his heart.

The Cowherd and the Weaving Maiden

China

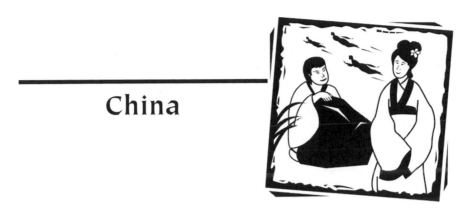

Long ago, there was a young man named Cheng. Cheng was a cowherd. His cow was a fairy beast that had the power of talking.

They were sitting on the grassy bank overlooking the river. Suddenly, Cheng heard laughter and splashing. He saw maidens dancing in the water.

The cow said, "Those are the seven maidens from the Heavenly Kingdom. Their beauty knows no match. But the fairest of the maidens is the Weaving Maiden. She weaves the sunset into the clouds and uses threads of silver and gold."

Cheng looked longingly at the maidens. He wished he could join them. He was lonely.

The cow said, "Cheng, I know that you are lonely. You need to take a wife. Tomorrow, return to this river. The heavenly maidens shed their robes and swim every day. Without their robes, they are unable to fly back to their kingdom."

So the next day, Cheng saw the heavenly maiden splashing in the river. He quietly stole the Weaving Maiden's red robe. When it was time to leave, her sisters donned their robes and flew to the sky.

23

The Weaving Maiden looked for her robe but could not find it. Cheng stepped out of the bushes with her robe. When the Weaving Maiden saw Cheng's kind and handsome face, she did not mind staying behind.

The Weaving Maiden fell in love with Cheng and remained on Earth as his wife. Together they had two children, and all was well for a time.

But one day, the Empress of Heaven discovered the spinning loom empty. For three years, the Weaving Maiden had abandoned her duties. None of the other sisters had the gift of weaving like their sister.

The clouds, once shades of golden pink and silvery blue, were now dull and gray. The Weaving Maiden had a special touch that brought the silken clouds to life. The Empress of Heaven was furious.

The Empress flew down to Earth and scooped up the Weaving Maiden. The Weaving Maiden's children cried, "Mama, mama!" but the Empress took her away, high in the sky.

When the cowherd returned from his work, he saw his children crying. He asked, "Where is your mother?" They told him about how their mother was taken to the sky.

The cowherd and his children were so sad. There was no way they could fly to the sky to see the Weaving Maiden.

The old cow spoke, "Fear not, cowherd, for I have a plan. Climb upon my back, and I will take you to the Heavenly Kingdom."

So the cowherd and his two children climbed upon the cow's back. The cow jumped up and began flying to the Heavens.

When they arrived, the children saw their mother weaving the magical colors into the clouds. They ran into her arms and cried, "Mama! Mama!"

The cowherd hugged the Weaving Maiden and begged her to come home. She said, "I cannot. I am bound by my duties. I do not have the power to leave."

Just then, the Empress of Heaven saw them. She cried out angrily, "How dare you enter the Heavenly Kingdom!"

She created a river of stars to separate Cheng and his children from the Weaving Maiden.

Cheng and his children cried. Tears fell from the eyes of the Weaving Maiden and created a storm cloud that rained heavily upon the Earth.

When the Empress of Heaven saw how sad the family was, she softened. She, too, had a soft spot in her heart for love.

She declared, "The Weaving Maiden cannot forsake her duties, but I will permit her to visit her Earth family on the Seventh Day of Seventh Moon."

So on the Seventh Day of the Seventh Moon, the Weaving Maiden is reunited with her family. When she sees her husband, Cheng, and her two children, she wraps her arms around them and weaves a silken blanket of love.

In China, they celebrate the Double Seventh. It takes place on the Seventh Day of the Seventh Moon. It is special day in the Chinese lunar calendar, which follows the phases of the moon.

On a clear night, you can see the stars of the Weaving Maiden and the stars of the Cowherd and his children. They move closer and closer together. When they are very close, you will know that it is time to celebrate the Double Seventh.

King Crocodile

Malaysia

Long ago, there lived a man named Hafiz who was famous for curing the sick. One evening, he met an old man sitting beside the road.

The old man cried, "Please help my daughter. She has a fishbone stuck in her throat. If you save her life, I will give you as much gold as you can carry from my palace."

Hafiz thought, "Palace? Gold?! I will be rich!" He said to the old man, "Yes, I will help you. Lead the way."

Hafiz was surprised to see the old man change into a crocodile. The crocodile said, "Do not worry. I will not harm you. Hop on my back and I will take you to my kingdom. I am the king of crocodiles."

Hafiz was alarmed. He cried out, "I cannot breathe under water, and my medicine is for humans!"

King Crocodile replied, "My magic will protect you underwater. At home, we are humans. We only become crocodiles to swim in the river or bask in the sun. We must hurry or my daughter will die."

Hafiz was afraid but the thought of gold comforted him. He climbed onto King Crocodile's back and they dove into the water. Soon, Hafiz was in a bejeweled palace at the bottom of the river.

The king of the crocodiles removed his crocodile skin and became an old man dressed in fine silk clothes. He summoned his strong and handsome son, the prince.

They led Hafiz to a room where the princess lay on a sofa clutching her throat. When Hafiz examined her, he found that a golden hairpin, not a fishbone, was stuck in her throat. He carefully removed the hairpin.

The princess sat up and took a deep breath. She was cured! King Crocodile was pleased. He and the prince took Hafiz to the treasure room. "Take as much treasure as you can carry," said King Crocodile.

Hafiz untied his head cloth and filled it with gold and jewels. He also stuffed as much gold as he could into his pockets. When Hafiz finished, he could hardly walk because of the weight of the treasure.

King Crocodile said, "My son will return you to the riverbank. Now, you must promise never to tell anyone about this. As long as you keep this secret, the crocodiles will be your friends. But if you break your promise, beware!"

Hafiz promised and the prince returned Hafiz to the riverbank. It wasn't long before the people of Hafiz's village began to question his sudden wealth. The village chief demanded that Hafiz share his story.

Hafiz had no choice. He told the chief about the King of the Crocodiles, the prince, and the princess. The chief thought, "If Prince Crocodile marries my daughter, they will have to pay a large dowry, and we will be rich!"

King Crocodile visited Hafiz's village often. He often spoke to the chief, and they became friends. Soon, the chief was invited to King Crocodile's palace. He brought his daughter dressed in the finest clothes she owned.

The prince fell in love with the chief's daughter. King Crocodile said, "My son the prince wants to marry your daughter. Chief, will you permit the wedding of our children?"

The chief said, "Yes, but the dowry must be enough gold to fill my rice container." King Crocodile agreed.

A few days later, King Crocodile and the prince returned with gifts of silk, jewels, and gold. But there was not enough gold to fill the rice container. No matter how much gold they put in, the container never filled.

King Crocodile became angry. "What is wrong with this container?" he cried, swinging his arm. He accidentally knocked over the container. It was then that the king and his son discovered the fraud.

There was a small hole in the bottom of the rice container and beneath that, a large box filled with the gold from their palace. King Crocodile was furious at being tricked.

He summoned all the crocodiles from the kingdom beneath the river. The crocodiles swallowed everyone in the village including the chief and his daughter. Although Hafiz begged for mercy, they swallowed him too for betraying their trust and spilling their secret.

The king, angry that he was betrayed, declared war against humans. Since that time, crocodiles no longer take their human shapes. They live in their watery kingdom below the river. When the crocodiles do surface, they are wary and on the lookout for humans.

If you happen to be in a river inhabited by crocodiles, watch out. King Crocodile is still angry, and if he sees you, he may just SNAP!

The Girl Who Used Her Wits

China

There was once a family with a father, his three sons, and his two daughters-in-law. The two daughters-in-law had just married the two oldest sons.

They soon grew homesick, and they pestered their father-in-law to grant permission to visit their mother.

The old man said, "I am tired of your constant begging. You have barely been married to my sons and yet you wish to return home. You may leave only if each of you brings me fire wrapped in paper and wind wrapped in paper. If you fulfill your tasks, you may leave as often as you wish. If you fail, you may never return here."

The two girls hastily agreed and chattered happily as they traveled home to their mother's house. Suddenly, they realized their folly.

It was an impossible task! Who could wrap wind or fire in paper?! They sat down by the side of the road and began to cry.

Just then, a young peasant girl was riding by on her horse. She stopped and asked, "Why are you crying?"

The two noble wives told her the whole story, and the peasant girl said, "That is not so bad. There is a simple solution. Come with me."

The peasant girl brought the two noble wives to her house. She made a paper lantern and handed it to the first wife. "This is fire wrapped in paper."

Then the peasant girl created a beautiful fan. She handed the paper fan to the second wife. "This is wind wrapped in paper."

The two wives thanked the young girl and dashed home, excited that their solution was so simple. When they showed the old man their objects, he said, "I have been outwitted! Who did this?"

The two wives told him about the young peasant girl. The old man said, "If that girl is so wise, then she needs to marry my youngest son."

So the girl who used her wits married the noble man's youngest son. The old man was so impressed by her wisdom that he made her the head of the house.

One day, a stranger came by and saw a great pile of stones in their yard. In that heap, he spotted a large jade of great value. He wanted the jade, so he asked to speak to the head of the house. When the young woman appeared, he was surprised but began bargaining.

He offered a large sum of money for the stones, saying he would use the stones for building a house. She agreed to sell the rocks, and the man said he would return two days later to haul them away. The young woman wondered why he wanted the stones and searched through the rocks. At once, she found the jade.

When the man returned, the young woman said, "I found the valuable jade in the pile of rocks. If you want the jade you must pay me the original price you offered for the rocks as well as a new price for the jade."

The man saw that he was outwitted and agreed. With their newfound wealth, the young woman and her family built a new house. Over the door of their house were the words, "No sorrow."

The emperor was passing by when he noticed the inscription. He asked to speak with the head of the house and was surprised to see the young woman appear. He said, "No house is without sorrow. I will fine you for your impudence. Weave me a cloth as long as this road."

The young woman replied, "I shall weave you your cloth as soon as you find the two ends of the road and tell me how many feet it is."

The emperor realized he had been outwitted. "Very well. Then I shall fine you as much oil as there is water in the sea."

The young woman replied, "When you tell me how many gallons of water the ocean contains, then I will gladly provide you with as much oil."

Again, the emperor was outwitted. "Very well. Since you are so quick-witted and able to read my mind, I will not fine you if you can tell me this: This quail in my hand—do I mean to squeeze it or set it free?"

The young woman answered, "Emperor, you have no right to fine me at all. But if you can answer my question, I will answer yours and pay your fine."

The emperor smiled as he sat in his sedan chair. The young woman said, "I am standing with one foot inside my house and one foot outside. Am I coming or going?"

The emperor did not know the answer. Since he had been outwitted, he agreed not to charge any fines to the girl who had used her wits.

The emperor bid her farewell and continued his journey. The young woman and her family prospered and lived happily the rest of their days because of her ability to use her wits.

The Crab and the Monkey

Japan

Crab and Monkey were great friends. One day, they saw each other as they were out for a walk. Crab had a rice cake, and Monkey had a persimmon seed. When Monkey saw Crab's rice cake, he became jealous. He was hungry and wanted to eat the rice cake.

Monkey spoke, "Crab, we should make a trade—my persimmon seed for your rice cake. Once you eat the rice cake, it is gone. But with a persimmon seed, you can grow an entire tree and have persimmons for the rest of your life!"

Crab thought it was a good idea, so he traded his rice cake for Monkey's persimmon seed. As soon as Monkey received the rice cake, he gobbled it up.

Crab took the persimmon seed home and planted it. With patience and careful tending, the tiny seed became a big tree full of ripe persimmons. But Crab had a problem. He was unable to climb to the top of the tree to pick the persimmons.

Crab called his friend, Monkey. "Will you please climb my persimmon tree and pick some of the sweet fruit for me?"

Monkey thought of the delicious persimmons and said, "Of course, my friend. I will be happy to help."

Monkey scampered to the top of the tree and sat in the branches. He began picking the ripe persimmons and eating them. Monkey threw the hard green persimmons at Crab, hitting him on top of the head.

Once Monkey finished eating all the ripe fruit, he climbed down. Crab was angry, but he had a plan to get back at Monkey. Crab asked his friends, Hornet, Chestnut, and Stone Mortar, to help him. The next day, Crab invited Monkey over for tea.

Monkey sat down near the fire. "Crab, you make the most delicious tea, and I loved your persimmons." The mention of persimmons angered Crab, and he gave his friends the signal.

Chestnut, who had been roasting in the fire, burst out of the fireplace and burned monkey's tail. Hornet flew down and stung Monkey on the nose. Monkey jumped up to run outside, but Stone Mortar was sitting above the door and fell down on top of Monkey's head, giving him a huge lump!

Monkey saw that there was no escape, so he bowed low before Crab. "I am sorry for stealing your ripe persimmons and throwing the hard green ones at you. I promise never to do such a thing again. Please forgive me."

Crab accepted Monkey's apology, and they were friends once more. Monkey learned his lesson and never again tried to trick his friend.

The Hermit
and the Worms

Philippines

In a time of great magic, there lived a wise old hermit. His hair was white, and his beard hung down to his knees. He spent most of his time praying and meditating in a dark cave on the slope of a mountain.

One day, he came out of his cave to gather wild fruit to eat. Just outside his cave, underneath a rotting log in the moist soil, lived two fat wriggling worms. As the hunched hermit began walking, he heard a voice yell, "Watch out! You will step on us!"

The old hermit looked around but did not see anyone. "Down here, old man," said the voice. The hermit bent down and saw the two worms. One of them spoke. "You nearly crushed us. You go about your business without noticing the world around you. You humans are uncaring and selfish."

"It is not so!" cried the hermit. "Perhaps there is something I can do for you. I will change you into people so that you can teach other humans how to care about the world. You can spread messages of kindness and compassion."

The worms agreed to the plan and with a wave of his hand, the hermit turned the two worms into a man and a woman. The old man called them Juan and Juanita. He gave them his blessing and said, "Go and live among the people. Do not forget your mission."

Juan and Juanita became husband and wife. They cultivated a small patch of land and built a modest house. After harvesting the fine crops that grew on their farm, the couple became wealthy after just a few seasons. At first, they treated everyone with kindness and gave to those in need. But soon greed took over.

In a few short years, they became the wealthiest people in town. They built a mansion and hired servants. Their house was the largest in the province. It was surrounded by a tall wall and golden gates. Don Juan and Doña Juanita wore jewels and expensive clothing and made friends only with other wealthy people.

They treated people poorly and kept all their money to themselves. The more they made, the more they wanted. There was never enough gold to satisfy Don Juan and Doña Juanita.

One day, they threw a lavish party for their rich friends. A servant came to Doña Juanita and said, "There is a beggar at the gate and he will not leave. We have offered him food and money but still, he will not leave. He insists on seeing you and Don Juan."

"Can't you see that I am busy?" said Doña Juanita irritably. "Send the dogs to chase him away. I don't have time for beggars."

"Doña Juanita, we have already sent the dogs and they came back whimpering. I am afraid that he will stay there all night."

The mistress was annoyed. "Fine. Don Juan and I will send him away ourselves."

So Don Juan and Doña Juanita left their party and walked to the gate. "What do you want, old beggar?" asked Don Juan.

"I wish to be invited into your house as a guest," said the old man with white hair and a beard that hung to his knees.

Doña Juanita placed her hands on her hips and said harshly, "We don't have time for people like you."

"You must leave at once," ordered Don Juan.

The old beggar said, "Perhaps if you lived as you had before, you would have time to think about people like me for I am the old hermit who gave two worms a chance at life as humans. You forgot your mission and have become the uncaring and selfish humans you despised just a few years ago."

Doña Juanita cried out, "No, please. We are sorry! We will change. Please don't take everything away!"

But it was too late. With a wave of his hand, the mansion, the tall wall, and the golden gates disappeared. Don Juan and Doña Juanita found themselves in the soft dirt as they were before … two fat, wriggling worms.

Lazybones

Laos

There was once a man so lazy that everyone called him Lazybones. His mornings, afternoons, and nights were spent lazing around. No one had ever seen him work a day in his entire life.

Lazybones lived under a wild fig tree. He was so lazy that he wouldn't even reach up to grab a fig. He would simply open his mouth and wait for the figs to fall in. The townspeople would say,

> Sitting around all day is just plain crazy
>
> Oh, Lazybones why are you so lazy?

He would answer, "While you are living a life of hard work, I am living a life of leisure," and he would continue to laze around.

One day, a mighty wind blew some of his wild figs into the river. The figs floated downriver. The king's daughter was sitting on the riverbank when she spotted the floating figs. She reached in and grabbed a few.

The princess ate one of the figs and exclaimed, "These are the most delicious fruit I have ever tasted! I shall marry the man who owns this fruit!"

She showed the king the figs and told him her plans. The king ordered everyone with figs to come to the castle so that his daughter could taste the fruit.

Each time someone presented the princess with figs, she would shake her head no and say,

> Though these figs are good to eat
>
> The figs I want are perfect and sweet

Meanwhile, Lazybones continued his daily routine. He lay under his fig tree, opened his mouth, and waited for the figs to fall in.

When the princess turned all the figs away, the king was determined to find out who owned the figs his daughter loved so much. He asked everyone he knew if there were figs in the land that had not been sampled by the princess.

Someone said, "Your Highness, the figs your daughter seeks belong to Lazybones. He doesn't work at all. He lives under his fig tree, opens his mouth, and waits for the figs to fall in. He was too lazy to make the journey to the castle."

When the princess heard this, she decided to visit Lazybones herself. She found his village and asked the people about him. They answered,

> Sitting around all day is just plain crazy
>
> Oh, Lazybones he is so very lazy!

They told her where his fig tree was, and sure enough, he was lying under the tree with his mouth wide open waiting for the figs to fall in.

The princess reached up and grabbed some figs. When she tasted them, she exclaimed,

> These figs are delicious and sweet
>
> These are the figs I want to eat!

She told Lazybones of her search and her desire to marry him. Since he was too lazy to go to church to get married, Lazybones and the princess were married right under the fig tree.

When the king found out the princess married someone so lazy, he banished her from the kingdom. Though the princess was sad that her father was upset, she lived in contentment with Lazybones under the big fig tree. They lay under the tree, opened their mouths, and waited for the figs to fall in.

They were happy for a time, but suddenly, tragedy struck. The princess had grown used to eating the figs, and they gave her good health. When the fig tree stopped bearing fruit, the princess became very sick.

Lazybones realized that he loved his wife very much and would do anything to nurse her back to health. He got up and began working. He planted new fig trees. The trees began growing, and the land prospered.

Once the princess had her fill of the delicious figs, she recovered. Once again, Lazybones and his wife were happy.

Word reached the king of Lazybones' efforts to nurse his daughter back to health. He welcomed her and her new husband back into the kingdom.

From that time on, Lazybones lived in the lap of luxury. And though he could live a life of leisure in the castle, he chose to work for the things that mattered most. He continued to plant fig trees and harvest its delicious fruit for his wife.

> Sitting around all day is just plain crazy
>
> Oh, Lazybones, he works and is no longer lazy!

The Legend
of the Lion City

Singapore

Many moons ago, there lived a king named Sang Nila Utama. He loved travel, hunting, and adventure. He heard that there was good hunting in the jungles of Tanjong Bentam and so he set sail.

When the king arrived on the island, he spotted a mighty stag. He drew his silver dagger and hurled it at the animal, but it was fleet of foot and ran swiftly away. The stag ran through the jungle to the top of a hill.

The king chased the stag up the hill, but when he reached the summit, the stag was nowhere to be seen. On top of the hill was a large rock. The king climbed up and looked across the island to the vast sea.

In the distance, he saw a stretch of white sand. It was another island. He asked his closest advisor the name of the island. The advisor answered, "That is the land of Temasek, your Highness."

The king ordered, "Tell the men to prepare to sail. We are going to Temasek."

The king and his men set sail toward the island. All at once, the skies darkened and lightning ripped across the sky. Thunder bellowed and the winds wailed. Rain and waves battered the ship.

King Sang Nila Utama's ship began taking in water. The men bailed furiously but the ship began to sink. The king ordered, "Throw our cargo overboard. Make our ship lighter."

The men began throwing large, heavy boxes overboard. But no matter how much they threw into the sea, the ship continued to be battered by the violent waves.

The king knew they had sailed into the heart of the storm and that the Sea King needed to be appeased. In desperation, the king threw his crown into the ocean as an offering and begged the Sea King to spare the ship.

Immediately, the storm broke. The skies cleared and once again the sun shone upon the king and his men. It seemed that the Sea King was happy with his new jeweled crown.

The ship made it to Temasek, and the king fell in love with the white sands and flowering plants. He was exploring the jungle when he came upon a majestic creature.

The animal had a black head with a furry mane, a white neck and chest, and a red body. It moved with grace and stared at the king with fierce golden eyes. The king was awestruck by the gigantic beast.

The beast shook his head and roared. He leaped over the stunned king and disappeared into the jungle. When the king described the creature to his advisor, his advisor said, "Your majesty, you must have seen a Singa, a lion. You could have been killed. It is a sign of good luck. The Singa has blessed you."

The king was so impressed with the majestic beast that he said, "I wish to make this island my new home. I wish to live in the land of the great Singa." The king gave the island a new name, Singa Pura, or Lion City, in honor of the great beast who blessed the king.

Little One-Inch

Japan

There was once a sweet old couple that wished, more than anything, to have a child. One day, after they went to the shrine and prayed, they heard a tiny cry coming from a clump of grass. When they looked down, they found a teeny tiny baby boy wrapped in a cherry red blanket.

The baby was so small, he was no bigger than a person's thumb! The woman exclaimed joyfully, "He is the answer to our prayers. We shall call him Little One-Inch."

When Little One-Inch grew older, he said to his parents, "You have given me much love and raised me well, but it is time that I explore the world and make my own fortune." Though his parents were sad, they helped Little One-Inch prepare for his journey.

They gave him a needle to use as a sword, a wooden rice bowl to use as a boat, and a chopstick to use as an oar. With his needle sword at his side, Little One-Inch waved goodbye to his parents and floated down the river in his rice bowl boat, paddling with his chopstick.

After floating for many miles, his boat was turned over by a frog. Little One-Inch swam to the bank and found himself before a great lord's house. He called out and a manservant came to the door. The servant looked around but did not see anyone.

"Down here!" cried Little One-Inch. "Look down here!" When the servant looked down, he saw Little One-Inch standing on top of the lord's wooden sandals. The servant brought him before the lord of the house.

"Well, well. What have we here?" asked the lord.

Standing straight and tall, Little One-Inch replied, "I am Little One-Inch, and I wish to become one of your warriors. I may be tiny, but I am strong."

The lord was impressed with Little One-Inch's bold words. "I shall make you the personal guard of my daughter, the princess." The princess and Little One-Inch soon became the best of friends.

One day, the princess and Little One-Inch went to visit a nearby temple. Suddenly, a terrible green ogre jumped out from behind the bushes and began chasing the princess.

Little One-Inch drew his sword and stuck the ogre's toes. It only made the ogre angrier. The ogre picked up Little One-Inch and swallowed him whole. "Oh no!" cried the princess. "Poor Little One-Inch!"

But Little One-Inch was strong and clever. He began pricking the inside of the ogre with his needle sword over and over. The ogre was in so much pain that he spit out Little One-Inch and ran away. As the ogre fled, his magic hammer fell to the ground.

The princess ran and picked up the hammer. "Little One-Inch, with the ogre's magic hammer, we can make a wish. What do you wish?"

Little One-Inch smiled, "I wish to grow to full size."

The princess waved the magic hammer in the air and sang, "Little One-Inch is mighty but small, please let him grow so he can be tall."

With every wave of the hammer, Little One-Inch grew, inch by inch by inch, until he was a full-size warrior. The princess jumped up and down with joy.

They ran home to her father, and the lord was pleased with Little One-Inch. The tiny but strong warrior had saved his daughter's life. Little One-Inch and the princess were married, and they lived a happy life, never to be bothered by ogres again.

The Magic Brocade

China

Long ago in China, there lived a mother and her three sons. She was a widow and had to support her boys, so she began weaving brocades. Over the years, she grew very skillful. Her brocades were made of rich fabric with threads of silver, gold, and silk. The weaver soon became famous, for she had a special gift of making flowers and birds appear as lifelike as life itself.

One day, the woman sold her brocades at the market. On her way home, she saw a breathtaking painting. It was a painting of a large field with a white house in the middle. It was filled with beautiful gardens, trees heavy with ripe fruit, and colorful birds. She was so enchanted by the painting that she bought it. When she arrived home, she showed the painting to her three sons.

She exclaimed, "If only we could live in such a place!"

The eldest son scoffed, "That is but a silly dream, mother."

The second eldest son also laughed, "You shouldn't fill your head with such nonsense!"

The youngest son offered comfort. "Mother, perhaps you could weave a brocade like the painting. It will be almost as nice as actually being there."

The woman smiled. "Thank you. That is just what I will do." She began weaving and barely stopped to take a rest. She wove late into the night and in the early morning. She wove although her back ached and her eyes burned. She would not stop.

The elder sons complained, "Mother you weave all day and night and never sell anything. We have to work so hard chopping wood to sell to feed us all!"

But the youngest son did not want his mother to worry. "It is okay. I will chop enough wood for us all." And he did.

Day after day, night after night, the woman continued her weaving. A year passed. Tears from her eyes dropped onto the brocade and formed a sparkling pond. Another year passed. Blood from her eyes dropped onto the brocade and produced fiery red flowers. Finally, at the end of the third year, the woman's brocade was finished. She stepped back to admire her work when a sudden wind picked up the brocade, and carried it out of the window. With a loud cry, she followed the brocade. But it was too late. It disappeared over the horizon. Frantically, she searched for her beautiful treasure but it was nowhere to be found. It had vanished.

Heartbroken, the weaver became sick and begged her sons, "Please find my treasure. It means more to me than anything. I put my soul into that brocade!"

The eldest journeyed to find the brocade. He came to a mountain pass where an old, white-haired woman sat in front of a stone horse. She asked him, "Are you looking for the beautiful brocade?"

"Yes," he answered. "I will do anything to get it back."

The old woman said, "Maybe you will and maybe you won't. The fairies have stolen your mother's brocade. They find it so beautiful that they are copying the design. If you want to find the brocade, you must put your two front teeth in the stone horse's mouth so he will come to life. After he eats ten pieces of red fruit from this tree, climb upon him. He will take you to Sun Mountain, where the fairies live. But first, you must pass through Flame Mountain and then cross the Sea of Ice. If you shudder even the slightest, the horse will turn back into stone and you will perish."

The eldest son became afraid. Just the thought of fiery flames and the icy sea made him shudder. He did not want to go.

The old woman laughed. "I can see already that you will not be able to stand the journey. Take this box of gold and live comfortably."

The eldest son took the gold and went happily on his way. When he did not return home, the weaver became more ill. So the second eldest journeyed to find the brocade. He came to the same mountain pass where the old, white-haired woman sat in front of a stone horse. She asked him, "Are you looking for the beautiful brocade?"

"Yes," he answered. "I will do anything to get it back."

The old woman said, "Maybe you will and maybe you won't." Just as she told his brother before him, she explained the tasks. The second eldest son became afraid. Just the thought of fiery flames and the icy sea made him shudder. He did not want to go.

The old woman laughed. "I can see already that you will not be able to stand the journey. Take this box of gold and live comfortably."

When the second eldest son did not return home, the woman grew deathly ill. So the youngest son journeyed to find the brocade. He came to the same mountain pass where the old, white-haired woman sat in front of a stone horse. She asked him, "Are you looking for the beautiful brocade?"

"Yes," he answered. "I will do anything to get it back."

The old woman said, "Maybe you will and maybe you won't. The fairies have stolen your mother's brocade. They find it so beautiful that they are copying the design. If you want to find the brocade you must put your two front teeth in the stone horse's mouth so he will come to life. After he eats ten pieces of red fruit from this tree, climb upon him. He will take you to Sun Mountain, where the fairies live. But first, you must pass through Flame Mountain and then cross the Sea of Ice. If you shudder even the slightest, the horse will turn back into stone and you will sink to the bottom."

Without thinking twice, the youngest son took out his two front teeth. He placed them in the stone horse's mouth, and it came to life. After the horse ate ten red fruit from the tree, the youngest son mounted the horse, and it sped away to Flame Mountain. Red and gold flames danced wildly. The boy urged his horse through the red-hot flames.

Once through the flames, they came to the Sea of Ice. The young man felt the cold squeezing his lungs. But he spurred his horse on, and they traveled across the sea. Though the cold numbed him through and through, he did not even shudder the slightest. When he emerged on the other side, he saw Sun Mountain.

They sped up the mountainside until he was at the door of a great palace. He entered and walked down a long hallway. At the end, he found shimmering fairies sitting at a loom, copying his mother's brocade. One spoke and said, "We are nearly finished copying your mother's brocade. Stay the night and we will return it to you tomorrow."

The young man sat down. The fairies fed him, and he felt refreshed. Finally, his eyes grew heavy and he fell asleep. One of the fairies was so sad that she had to part with the original brocade, she embroidered a picture of herself into it. When the young man awoke, he found the brocade hanging on the wall. He carefully wrapped it up and tied it to his body. He mounted his horse and galloped away.

Again, he traveled through the Sea of Ice and Flame Mountain. At the mountain pass, the old, white-haired woman greeted him with a smile. The young man removed his front teeth from the horse, and it turned back into stone. "What courage you have, young man," she said as she handed him a pair of embroidered slippers. "Wear these, and they will bring you home swiftly."

He thanked the old woman and donned the slippers. Soon, he was home. His mother was in bed, her face pale and her eyes closed. "Mother," he whispered in her ear, "I have your brocade!"

Immediately, her eyes fluttered open. As soon as she saw the brocade, her strength returned. She jumped out of bed and said, "Let us unroll this treasure outside!"

When they unrolled the brocade, a strange and magical thing happened. The threads of the brocade trembled and a large field with a white house appeared. Flower-filled gardens came to life. The trees were heavy with ripe fruit and colorful birds flew above. It was exactly as the woman had woven it except for one thing. Standing near the shimmering fishpond was a beautiful girl in red. It was the fairy who had embroidered herself into the brocade.

The kind woman was thrilled with her good fortune. The beautiful fairy girl and the youngest son were married, and they all lived happily ever after.

The Magic Paper Charms

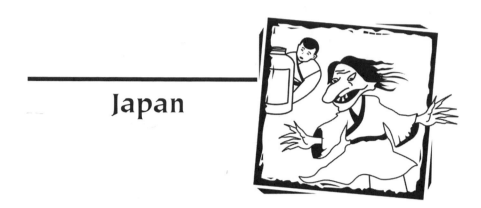

Japan

Once there was a wise old priest and his apprentice who lived in a mountain temple. The apprentice was a young mischievous boy who did not always listen to his master. The master warned him, "Do not climb up the mountain too far, for the Yamanba lives there, a terrible magical mountain woman. She will catch you and eat you up!"

The boy laughed and said, "There is no such thing as a Yamanba, old man. That is just a wives' tale."

The priest shook his head at the boy. "Just in case, you better take these magic paper charms. Should you ever meet the Yamanba, you may need them." The boy took the charms from the old priest and stuffed them in his robe pocket, forgetting about them.

One day the boy saw some delicious chestnut trees up the mountain. He loved chestnuts and climbed up the mountain to gather them. He heard a noise behind him and turned to see a kind old woman.

She smiled at him and said, "The chestnuts are ripe and delicious, but they need to be cooked. Why don't you come to my house and I will cook them for you." The old woman looked harmless, so the boy agreed.

When they arrived, the old woman cooked the chestnuts, and the boy greedily ate them. He filled his stomach and became sleepy. He yawned and fell asleep.

A few hours later when the boy awoke, he peeked into the next room and saw a terrible mountain woman hunched over a large pot! Her face was yellow, her eyes were red, and her tangled white hair stuck out everywhere. She had long nails and sharp teeth. It was the Yamanba!

"Oh no!" the boy cried out. "The old man was right!" The Yamanba turned and looked at the boy.

"So you have discovered me! Never mind. You will make a very tasty dinner!" She slurped as she added spices to the pot.

The boy had to think fast. "I have to go to the bathroom," he said. He crossed his legs and began to dance around.

"Very well," said the Yamanba impatiently. "But I shall see that you do not escape!" She tied a strong rope around his waist, and he went into the bathroom.

"I should have listened to my master!" said the boy. "Now I am in big trouble! I better come up with a plan!"

The Yamanba called, "Are you done yet?"

"Just a minute. I'll be out soon," answered the boy. It was then that he remembered the magic paper charms the old priest had given him. He had an idea. He pulled out one of the charms and stuck it to the wall.

"Magic charm, please pretend to be me when she calls." The boy untied the rope, climbed out of the window and ran as fast as he could.

The Yamanba called again, "Are you done yet?"

"Just a minute. I'll be out soon," answered the magic paper charm, sounding just like the boy. The Yamanba kept calling for the boy, and the paper charm continued giving the same answer. Becoming suspicious, the Yamanba finally looked into the bathroom. "The boy is gone! He tricked me!" She ran after the boy.

Although the boy had run far, the Yamanba was faster. Soon she was right behind him. "Oh no!" cried the boy. He pulled out the second magic paper charm and threw it behind him. "Magic paper charm, become a river!"

A roaring river rushed between the Yamanba and the boy. But she too had her own magic. She opened her mouth and sucked up the river. Soon, she was right behind him again. "Oh no!" cried the boy. He pulled out the third magic paper charm and threw it behind him. "Magic paper charm, become fire!"

A blazing fire created a wall between the Yamanba and the boy. But she blew the river out of her mouth and put out the fire. The boy arrived at the temple door and shouted, "Master, master, please let me in. The Yamanba is going to get me! You were right! I promise to listen to you from now on!"

The priest opened the door and let the boy in. The boy hid inside a jar. When the Yamanba arrived, she asked, "Where is that boy who ran in here?"

The old priest answered, "There is no boy."

"Fine. I know you are hiding him, but I will eat you instead," said the Yamanba.

"Why don't we play a game over some mochi, some sweet rice cakes?" asked the old man. The Yamanba licked her lips. She loved mochi, so she agreed.

As she stuffed a mochi into her big mouth, the old priest said, "I hear that you can turn yourself into anything you want. Can you turn yourself into something big like a mountain?"

The Yamanba laughed. "Of course I can. That is easy." In the blink of an eye, she grew larger and larger until she became a mountain.

The old man clapped his hands. "Most excellent. But I am sure that you cannot turn yourself into something tiny like a soybean."

The Yamanba laughed again. "Of course I can. That is easy." In the blink of an eye, she shrank smaller and smaller until she became a soybean.

And just like that, the old man picked up the soybean with his chopsticks and ate it up. Yummy in his tummy. From that time on, the young boy always listened to his master, and years later, he became a wise old priest himself.

The Magic Pot

China

Mr. and Mrs. Chin were old and poor. They had a small house in the mountains and a tiny patch of land on which they grew fruit and vegetables. Mr. Chin would harvest the produce and sell it at the market in the village.

One day, on his way home from the market, he saw a large black pot in the middle of the road. He said, "What a nice pot! Why, with this pot my wife could cook rice, with this pot my wife could stew, with this pot my wife could cook soup with noodles!"

It didn't seem to belong to anyone, so Mr. Chin carried the heavy pot home. When Mr. Chin arrived home, his wife greeted him at the door. He gave her the pot and said, "This nice pot is for you, dear wife."

Mrs. Chin was delighted. She said, "What a splendid pot. Why, with this pot I could cook rice, with this pot I could stew, with this pot I could cook soup with noodles!"

Mr. Chin groaned and rubbed his stomach. "Wife, please do not speak to me of food. I am so very hungry!"

Mrs. Chin said, "I have an idea. Why don't we use the pot now?! I will cook some rice." Mrs. Chin ran to the kitchen and returned with a bag of rice. She held the rice over the pot.

What Mr. and Mrs. Chin did not know was that the bag of rice had a small hole at the bottom. A single grain of rice fell into the pot. Mrs. Chin saw it fall and looked inside the pot. "Aaaah!" she screamed.

"Wife, wife, what is the matter?" cried Mr. Chin, thinking that something was wrong.

Mrs. Chin said, "We have a magic pot!"

Mr. Chin said, "That's ridiculous. It is an ordinary pot. How can it be magic?"

Mrs. Chin replied, "One grain of rice fell into the pot and two grains of rice came out! It is a magic pot that doubles everything you place inside it. I'll prove it." Mrs. Chin pulled a chopstick from her hair.

Lo and behold, one chopstick went into the pot and two chopsticks came out. Mr. Chin gasped. "It is a magic pot!"

Mrs. Chin was excited. "Husband," she said, "let us double everything we own!" They began placing objects inside the pot. One bowl went into the pot and two bowls came out. One mat went into the pot and two mats came out. One pillow went into the pot and two pillows came out!

After they had doubled most of their belongings, Mrs. Chin had a brilliant idea. She went to the back of the house and returned with a gold coin in her hand. One gold coin went into the pot and two gold coins came out!

She smiled at Mr. Chin and placed the two gold coins into the magic pot. Two gold coins went into the pot and four gold coins came out. Four gold coins went into the pot and eight gold coins came out.

Eight gold coins went into the pot and sixteen gold coins came out. Sixteen gold coins went into the pot and thirty-two gold coins came out. Thirty-two gold coins went into the pot and sixty-four gold coins came out.

Sixty-four cold coins went into the pot and one hundred twenty-eight gold coins came out! One hundred twenty-eight gold coins went into the pot and soon, there were too many gold coins to count! Mr. and Mrs. Chin were rich!

Mr. and Mrs. Chin put the magic pot away in the kitchen, but that night, Mrs. Chin could not sleep. She kept thinking about the magic pot! Early in the morning, she crept into the kitchen and pulled out the magic pot.

"Oh, magic pot. You have changed our lives for the better! I love you!" She bent over to hug the pot and suddenly, Mrs. Chin fell in! One Mrs. Chin went into the pot and two Mrs. Chins came out! They screamed!

Mr. Chin came running, and when he saw two Mrs. Chins, he screamed too! "I can barely handle one wife. How will I handle two?"

The two Mrs. Chins began to argue. The first Mrs. Chin said, "I was here first. You must leave!"

The second Mrs. Chin said, "He is my husband too, and I am here to stay!"

Mr. Chin yelled, "Please stop! Surely, there must be a solution to this problem!"

It was then that the first Mrs. Chin whispered into the ear of the second Mrs. Chin. They called Mr. Chin over, and when he was close to the pot, they pushed Mr. Chin in! One Mr. Chin fell into the pot and two Mr. Chins came out!

Both sets of Chins looked at each other, and that's when the first Mrs. Chin had another brilliant idea. With the gold from the magic pot, she built a house next door for the new couple. When the neighbors passed, they commented on how much they resembled each other. They said, "We must be seeing double Chins!"

The Magic Teakettle

Japan

There was once a priest who loved to drink tea. One day, in an old secondhand shop, he found a lovely iron teakettle. He brought it home and polished it. He put water into the kettle and placed it over the fire. "I can't wait to drink my tea," said the priest.

The fire blazed and the kettle became hotter and hotter and hotter until suddenly, a very odd thing happened. The kettle grew the head of a badger, four badger feet, and a big bushy badger tail.

The badger teakettle hopped off the fire and danced around. "Ooh, ooh, ooh, that is hot, hot, hot!" He began running out the door.

The old priest ran after him and caught the badger teakettle. As soon as he picked it up, it turned back into a regular iron teakettle. The priest said, "You must be a bewitched teakettle. I cannot have that kind of mischief in my temple."

So the priest found a junkman and sold the teakettle for a very small price. The junkman was pleased to have found such a bargain. He brought the teakettle home, polished it, and placed it in the middle of the table.

The kettle grew the head of a badger, four badger feet, and a big bushy badger tail. It spoke to the junkman, "Hello."

The junkman was startled. "Oh my goodness. Not only have you grown a head, legs, and a tail, but you can also talk!"

The badger teakettle said, "That's right. I am no ordinary teakettle. My name is Bumbuku, which means 'Good Luck.' The priest put me over a fire and burned me, so I tried to run away from him. If you treat me kindly, feed me rice cakes, and promise never to put me over a fire, I will make you a very rich man."

The junkman said, "I promise. But how will you do that?"

Bumbuku answered, "I can do all sorts of tricks and people will pay to see me perform!"

Bumbuku was right. People from all over the land paid to see Bumbuku, the Magic Teakettle of Good Luck perform. He balanced on a tight rope while fanning himself with one hand and eating rice cakes with the other. The people cheered and cheered for Bumbuku.

Bumbuku and the old junkman became good friends. As Bumbuku promised, the junkman became rich. One day, the junkman said, "Bumbuku, you have been so good to me. You must tire of doing these tricks every day. I have all I need now. Perhaps you should return to the temple and live the rest of your days peacefully."

Bumbuku cried out, "No, don't take me back there. The mean priest will burn me alive if he puts me over the fire!"

The junkman said, "Bumbuku, I will take care of everything. You will have no worries for the rest of your life."

The junkman went to the temple and told his story to the priest. The priest said, "If I had known Bumbuku was a magic teakettle of good luck, I would never have placed him over the fire. He is welcome to stay at the temple for as long as he likes."

So Bumbuku and the old junkman bid each other farewell. Bumbuku stayed at the temple. They never placed Bumbuku over the fire, and they fed him his favorite food, rice cakes. The old junkman often visited Bumbuku, and Bumbuku lived the rest of his days peacefully.

The Man in the Moon

Vietnam

In a small village of the eastern country, there lived a rich landowner who owned many fields. He had many servants working for him—among them, a young boy named Cuoi. Cuoi was kindhearted, hardworking, and always did what he was told. One day, he was asked to go into the forest to chop wood.

Cuoi lost his way as he daydreamed about becoming rich and taking a beautiful bride. It was then he saw a wounded baby tiger on the ground. Afraid that the cub's mother would find him, Cuoi hid in a nearby tree. The baby tiger groaned in pain.

Sure enough, the mother tiger returned to see her cub hurt and crying. She turned around and began walking toward Cuoi's tree. Cuoi was terrified. He thought he had been discovered and held his breath. To his surprise, the tigress walked past his tree to a tree behind him, climbed up the other tree, and bit off some leaves.

She returned to her baby cub and placed the leaves on its wound. Suddenly, the wound healed, and the baby tiger jumped up. Cuoi was astonished. It was a tree with magic leaves! When the tigress and her cub left, Cuoi climbed down from his tree and dug up the magic tree.

Cuoi planted the tree behind his house and took care of it, watering its roots with fresh clean water every day. He pulled off the leaves and made medicine with it. When he gave the medicine to sick people, they were healed immediately. Cuoi soon became a rich and famous doctor.

One day, Cuoi was traveling home when he wandered to a small spring. There, he saw a girl lying unconscious on the bank. Feeling sorry for her, he picked her up and brought her home. He nursed her back to health with the magic medicine from his tree. They fell in love and were married.

All was well except for one thing. Cuoi's wife could never remember the instructions her husband gave her. She would either forget them or misunderstand him entirely. One day, Cuoi was preparing to journey to the next village to tend to a sick man. He said, "Give my tree water, clean and fresh."

After Cuoi left, his wife tried to remember what he said. "What did he tell me to do? Oh yes! I remember now! He said, 'Give my tree garbage, it needs trash.' " So she brought the trashcan to the tree and dumped all the garbage onto its roots. Suddenly, the tree began to uproot and fly toward the sky.

Cuoi's wife screamed, "Help! Help! The tree is flying away!"

Cuoi was nearly home when he heard the cries and saw his tree flying up. He ran and jumped up. Cuoi managed to grab onto a root as the tree rose higher and higher.

His wife called out, "Cuoi, come down!"

But Cuoi could not let go. The tree was too high. He hung on and rose higher and higher until he reached the moon. The tree settled down and began growing right on top of the moon!

Soon after, a beautiful girl appeared. "I am the Moon Maiden. Welcome to your new home."

Although Cuoi missed his wife very much, he could not leave the moon. The moon was now his home. To this day, if you look at the moon, you can see Cuoi and his magic tree.

In Vietnam, when the moon is full in the middle of August, there is the Mid-Autumn Festival. Parents buy moon cakes and rice paper lanterns for their children. The children carry the lighted lanterns and celebrate the Autumn Festival with songs. They look up into the night sky and remember Cuoi and his magic tree. They see the man in the moon.

Momotaro, the Peach Boy

Japan

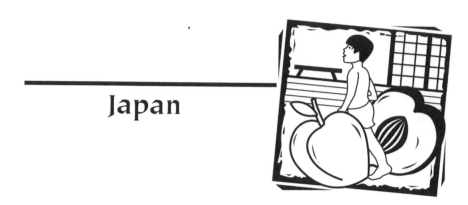

There once lived a kind woodcutter and his wife. More than anything, they prayed for a child. One day, when the woodcutter went into the forest to work, the old woman went to the river to wash clothes. As she was washing, she saw a giant peach floating down the river.

She reached in and pulled out the peach. "What a fine peach you are," she said. "My husband will be very pleased to see you."

She brought the giant peach home. The woodcutter was delighted, "We have been blessed. I cannot wait to taste this delectable fruit!"

He was about to carve the peach with a knife when a voice inside cried out, "Wait, don't cut me!"

The astonished woodcutter dropped his knife when the peach split apart and a little boy stood in front of him and his wife. The boy said, "I have been sent to you in answer to your prayers."

The woodcutter and his wife were delighted. They named the boy Momotaro, which means Boy-of-the-Peach. Momotaro grew up to be a fine young boy. When he was fifteen, he said, "Mother and father, you have been good parents. Now I must venture off on my own to help my country. Not far from here is Oni Island, the land of the ogres. I must find a way to defeat the Oni so that they will stop terrorizing our people."

Though the woodcutter and his wife were sad to see their son leave, they knew in their hearts that he would return. Before Momotaro left, his mother packed him some millet dumplings.

Momotaro began traveling to Oni Island. Along the way, he stopped for a bit to eat. As he ate his millet dumplings, he saw a spotted dog. The dog barked, "Rof, rof, rof!" Momotaro offered the dog his dumplings, and the dog ate happily.

When he finished eating, the dog asked, "Where are you going?"

Momotaro said, "I am going to Oni Island to defeat the ogres."

"Then I will come with you," said the dog. "You will need help."

They began traveling to Oni Island when they happened upon a monkey. The monkey chattered, "Kia, kia, kia!"

The spotted dog growled at the monkey, and the two began to quarrel. Momotaro said, "Stop it, both of you. We need to go."

The monkey asked, "Where are you going?"

Momotaro said, "We are going to Oni Island to defeat the ogres."

"Then I will come with you," said the monkey. "You will both need help."

They began traveling to Oni Island when a pheasant jumped out in front of them. The dog and the monkey were about to attack the pheasant when Momotaro said, "Stop it, all of you. Eat some millet dumplings. We need to go."

The animals happily gobbled up the millet dumplings. The pheasant asked, "Where are you going?

Momotaro said, "We are going to Oni Island to defeat the ogres."

"Then I will come with you," said the pheasant. "You will all need help."

During the journey, a strange thing happened. The three animals, who did not normally get along, became friends. They arrived at the sea's edge and Momotaro and the animals built a boat. They crossed the ocean to Oni Island, the land of the ogres.

As they approached the island, they saw the ugly ogres. Momotaro announced, "Surrender now before you regret it!"

The ogres laughed, "Ho, ho, ho, ho, ho! You will never defeat us, little boy, with your puny animal army! Ho, ho, ho, ho, ho!"

The ogres underestimated the power of determination. Momotaro and his friends charged the ogres. The pheasant pecked at them, the monkey scratched at them, and the dog bit their legs. Momotaro waved his sword high and asked, "Now will you surrender?"

The ogres wearily agreed that Momotaro and his animal friends had defeated them, and so the ogres surrendered and promised to stop terrorizing the people of Japan. They also presented Momotaro with the most wonderful treasure you can imagine: gold, silver, precious jewels, and magic objects.

Momotaro loaded their boat with the treasure and returned home. Momotaro and his friends were celebrated heroes. They had their friendship and all the millet dumplings they could eat. From that time on, their lives were just, well, peachy.

The Monkey
and the Crocodile

Philippines

Monkey lived in a great big, beautiful tree, and that tree was covered with his favorite fruit in the whole world—mangos. Monkey loved to eat the golden, ripe, and juicy mangos.

One day, crocodile swam downriver. He stopped in front of Monkey's tree. Monkey was eating a sweet, delicious mango when Crocodile asked, "Monkey, what are you doing?"

Monkey replied, "Ooooo, Aaaaaaa. I am eating mangos."

Crocodile asked, "Mangos? What's a mango?"

"A mango is a sweet, delicious fruit that is yummy in your tummy. Would you like to try one?"

Crocodile answered, "Uh-huh."

So Monkey reached up, grabbed a sweet, delicious mango, and threw it down to Crocodile. Crocodile ate the mango and said, "Mmmmm. Yummy. Do you have any more?"

Monkey reached up, grabbed another sweet, delicious mango, and threw it down to Crocodile. Crocodile ate the mango and said, "Mmmm. Yummy!" Every day, Crocodile would swim down river and say, "Hey monkey, do you have any mangos?"

Monkey would reach up, grab a sweet, delicious mango, and throw it down to Crocodile. Because Crocodile visited every day, he and Monkey became very good friends.

One day, Chief Crocodile found out that Crocodile was friends with Monkey. He devised a plan to get Monkey to the village. He pretended to be very sick. Crocodile asked, "What's wrong, Chief?"

The chief answered, "I am very sick. I need the heart of a monkey to get better. You must go and bring Monkey to the village. Tell him that we are having a party in his honor and invite him. Then swim him on your back here."

Crocodile and Monkey were friends and Crocodile did not want to bring Monkey to the village. But he did not dare disobey his chief.

So Crocodile swam down river. When he arrived at Monkey's tree, he shouted, "Hey, Monkey!"

Monkey poked his head out of the tree and answered, "Hi, Crocodile! Do you want a mango?"

Crocodile answered, "Actually, my chief sent me here to invite you to a party in your honor."

Monkey was excited. He jumped up and down. "Oooooo. Aaaaaaa. A party? I like parties." He climbed down the tree and stood in front of Crocodile. "But how will I get there? I cannot swim."

"You can hop on my back and I will swim you there," answered Crocodile.

So Monkey hopped onto Crocodile's back, and they began swimming up river. Then in the middle of the river Crocodile stopped. "Monkey, there's something I must tell you. My chief is not really throwing a party in your honor. He sent me to get you because he is sick and needs the heart of a monkey to cure him."

Monkey said, "The heart of a monkey? Really? I wish you'd told me that in the first place. I never travel with my heart. I left it up in my tree. If you swim me back to my tree, I'll go get it."

Crocodile answered, "Okay." And he swam down river, stopping in front of Monkey's tree. Monkey hopped off his back and climbed up the tree.

Crocodile waited and waited and waited. Finally, he called out, "Hey, Monkey!"

Monkey poked his head out of his tree, made a big monkey face, stuck his tongue out, and said, "Prrrrrrrr." He reached up, grabbed a sweet, delicious mango and threw it at Crocodile, hitting him square on the nose. "Take that to your chief! Who is the bigger fool now?"

Crocodile swam off, leaving Monkey in the mango tree. That is how Monkey outsmarted Crocodile. To this day, monkeys and crocodiles stay in their separate parts of the jungle. If you ever walk through the jungle, watch out. Because monkeys still throw things from the tops of the trees, thinking it might be a crocodile coming back to trick them.

The Mouse's Wedding

Japan

Long ago, there lived a rich mouse who had a beautiful daughter named Sachiko. Sachiko had a suitor, a handsome but poor mouse by the name of Makoto. Makoto wanted to marry Sachiko.

One day, Makoto came to visit the family. They sat at the table and drank tea. Father Mouse, "I wish to marry Sachiko. May I have your permission?"

Father Mouse laughed. "I am a rich mouse. My daughter cannot marry a common mouse like you. She must marry the mightiest creature in the world."

Makoto answered, "Father Mouse, I promise to work hard and give Sachiko everything that she needs." But Father Mouse would not hear of it and sent Makoto away.

Father Mouse spoke to his wife. "Wife, Sachiko has a suitor, a common mouse. But I cannot let my daughter marry unless she marries the mightiest creature in the world. Everyone knows the mightiest one is Mr. Sun."

Mother Mouse nodded. "Of course. Perhaps you should see him and ask him to marry our Sachiko." Father Mouse thought it was a good idea and set off to see the Sun.

When he arrived, he greeted the Sun with a bow. "Good day, Mr. Sun. I want my daughter to marry the mightiest creature in the world. Since you bring light to the world, you must be the mightiest."

The Sun smiled, "I am flattered but I am afraid I am not the mightiest. When Mr. Cloud passes by, he covers my face, therefore, he must be the mightiest."

Father Mouse thanked the Sun and continued on his journey. When he found the Cloud, he greeted him with a bow. "Good Day, Mr. Cloud. I want my daughter to marry the mightiest creature in the world. Since you cover Mr. Sun, you must be the mightiest."

The Cloud smiled, "I am flattered, but I am afraid I am not the mightiest. When Mr. Wind comes near, he blows me across the sky, therefore, he must be the mightiest."

Father Mouse thanked the Cloud and continued on his journey. When he found the Wind, he greeted him with a bow. "Good Day, Mr. Wind. I want my daughter to marry the mightiest creature in the world. Since you blow Mr. Cloud across the sky, you must be the mightiest."

The Wind smiled, "I am flattered, but I am afraid I am not the mightiest. When I approach Mr. Wall, he stops me in my tracks, therefore, he must be the mightiest."

Father Mouse thanked the Wind and continued on his journey. When he found the Wall, he greeted him with a bow. "Good Day, Mr. Wall. I want my daughter to marry the mightiest creature in the world. Since you stop Mr. Wind in his tracks, you must be the mightiest."

The Wall smiled, "I am flattered, but I am afraid I am not the mightiest. Do you see that hole in me? That hole is made by the mightiest creature around. He has the power to chew right through me!"

Father Mouse asked, "Honorable Mr. Wall, what creature has that kind of power?"

The Wall laughed. "Why, it's the mouse! You mice must be the mightiest and strongest creatures in the world!"

Father Mouse was surprised. He thanked the Wall and journeyed home. And you can guess what happened next! Father Mouse granted Makoto permission to marry Sachiko because the mouse was, after all, the mightiest creature in the world! And they lived happily ever after. Squeak! Squeak!

The Noble Frog

China

In Old Cathay, there lived a Chinese general and his wife. They prayed for a baby. It seemed as though their prayers were being answered, for the wife conceived and gave birth. But the birth was a great shock to everyone for she did not give birth to a baby but to a frog as large as an infant child!

The mother of the frog had no choice but to set him loose in the garden. He returned daily for his food and grew in size. The frog's father was away fighting a civil war. Word reached the family that he had been captured.

The frog spoke to his uncle. "Uncle, you must take me to the castle so that I may ask the emperor to help me save my father's life."

No sooner had they arrived at the castle when they heard the emperor decree, "Whoever banishes the rebels and sets my general free can marry Mei Ling, my only daughter."

Mei Ling was of uncommon beauty. The moon paled in comparison to her glowing splendor. She had a smile that stole many hearts.

When the frog saw Mei Ling, his heart leaped with joy. Not only would he defeat the enemies and bring his father home, he would also win the hand of the lovely princess!

The frog insisted on an audience with the emperor. When he was brought before the emperor, the frog bowed low. "Most honorable emperor, my father is the general of your army. He has been captured by enemy troops. I wish to free him and bring him home, but I request your help."

The emperor looked at the frog with disbelief. "How can you, a lowly frog, expect to defeat my enemy? Nevertheless, I will help you only because your father has given me many years of loyal service and I wish his safe return. I will give you a horse and a few soldiers. That is all."

The frog thanked the emperor and set off on his white horse with his tiny army. They traveled to the far region of the land and faced the emperor's enemy. When the enemy army saw the cavalry the emperor had sent, they roared with laughter. There was no way this tiny army and ridiculous frog on a white horse could defeat them.

They charged the frog and his army. The frog spit poison that rained upon his enemy. The poison paralyzed them and the frog and his soldiers rescued the general and the other imprisoned soldiers.

There was much rejoicing when the frog returned a hero. He had saved his father the general and freed the emperor's army. The frog said to the emperor, "You proclaimed that whoever freed the general and defeated the enemy could marry Mei Ling, your only daughter."

The emperor was aghast! There was no way he would allow an unsightly creature like this frog marry his daughter. Finally he said, "Come back tomorrow. If you can pick out my daughter from a group of maidens, you may have her hand in marriage."

That night the frog dreamed that the princess wore a yellow chrysanthemum in her hair. The next day, the emperor had Mei Ling and all the maidens dress alike. Mei Ling had placed a beautiful yellow chrysanthemum in her hair. The frog hopped to Mei Ling and tugged at her gown with his mouth.

The emperor was not happy but he had to keep his word. The frog asked for a suit to be made for the wedding, and the emperor scoffed, "What good will a suit do a frog?"

The frog answered, "The clothes make a man." So a suit was made for the frog. When the frog put on the suit, he shed his frog skin and became a dashing young man. Mei Ling was ecstatic. The frog man and Mei Ling were married.

The emperor couldn't understand how the young man fit into a frog's skin so he stole the skin and tried it on. Once he put the skin on, he was no longer able to take it off. The disbelieving emperor had no choice but to allow his new son-in-law to rule in his place.

From that moment forward, Mei Ling and her husband ruled wisely and justly. As for the old emperor, he became accustomed to his life as a frog and spent the rest of his days hopping happily about the palace gardens and sleeping on a grand lily pad. And they lived happily for the rest of their days.

The Purple Hen Sparrow

India

One day Hen Sparrow was sitting on the edge of a cloth maker's pot of dye. She fell in, and when she flew out, she was purple!

Hen Sparrow flew home unaware of her fate. When her husband, Cock Sparrow saw her, he was startled. Never before had he seen a purple bird. "Who are you?" he asked.

"It is I, Hen Sparrow," his wife answered. Cock Sparrow was shocked. He flew into a state of frenzy and became so upset that his feathers fell off. He flew to a nearby Pipal tree, sat on the branches, and cried.

Pipal asked, "Cock Sparrow, what is wrong?"

Cock Sparrow answered,

"Hen Sparrow is dyed purple, now I feel blue.

Tell me, tell me, what shall I do?"

Cock Sparrow's sadness became Pipal's sadness, and she, too, began crying. She was so upset that she dropped her leaves.

After a while, Buffalo came by to rest in the shade of Pipal's leaves. He was shocked to see that Pipal was bare.

Buffalo asked, "Pipal, what is wrong?"

Pipal answered,

"Hen Sparrow is dyed purple, now I feel blue

68

Tell me, tell me, what shall I do?

Cock Sparrow lost his feathers,

So I have dropped my leaves."

Pipal's sadness became Buffalo's sadness, and he, too, began crying. He was so upset that he cast his horns. After a while, he went for a drink from the river.

When River saw Buffalo without his horns, River asked, "Buffalo, what is wrong?"

Buffalo answered,

"Hen Sparrow is dyed purple, now I feel blue.

Tell me, tell me, what shall I do?

Cock Sparrow lost his feathers,

Pipal dropped her leaves,

So I have cast my horns."

Buffalo's sadness became River's sadness, and she, too, began crying. She was so upset that she became salty.

Soon after, Peacock came to the river for a drink. When he tasted the salty water, he asked, "River what is wrong?"

River answered,

"Hen Sparrow is dyed purple, now I feel blue,

Tell me, tell me, what shall I do?

Cock Sparrow lost his feathers,

Pipal dropped her leaves,

Buffalo cast his horns,

So I have become salty."

River's sadness became Peacock's sadness, and he too, began crying. He was so upset that he plucked his brilliant plume. He walked to the village and sat by the shopkeeper's store. When the shopkeeper saw Peacock without his plume, he asked, "Peacock, what is wrong?"

Peacock answered,

"Hen Sparrow is dyed purple, now I feel blue,

Tell me, tell me, what shall I do?

Cock Sparrow lost his feathers,

Pipal dropped her leaves,

Buffalo cast his horns,

River became salty,

So I have plucked my plume."

Peacock's sadness became the shopkeeper's sadness, and he, too, began crying. He wept and wailed until he lost his senses. The king's cook came to buy some pepper and curry, but the shopkeeper gave her garlic and rice. Seeing that the shopkeeper had lost his senses, the cook asked, "Shopkeeper, what is wrong?"

Shopkeeper answered,

"Hen Sparrow is dyed purple, now I feel blue.

Tell me, tell me, what shall I do?

Cock Sparrow lost his feathers,

Pipal dropped her leaves,

Buffalo cast his horns,

River became salty,

Peacock plucked his plume,

So I have lost my senses."

The shopkeeper's sadness became the cook's sadness, and she, too, began crying. The cook walked back to the palace. She moaned and she mourned. When the queen saw the cook's distress, she asked, "Cook, what is wrong?"

Cook answered,

"Hen Sparrow is dyed purple, now I feel blue.

Tell me, tell me, what shall I do?

Cock Sparrow lost his feathers,

Pipal dropped her leaves,

Buffalo cast his horns,

River became salty,

Peacock plucked his plume,

Shopkeeper lost his senses,

So I shed my tears."

The cook's sadness became the queen's sadness, and she, too, began crying. The queen danced until she was almost out of breath. When her son saw her dancing, he began drumming. When the king saw the prince drumming, he began strumming the zither. The cook began singing,

"Hen Sparrow is dyed purple, now we feel blue.

Tell us, tell us, what shall we do?

Cock Sparrow lost his feathers,

Pipal dropped her leaves,

Buffalo cast his horns,

River became salty,

Peacock plucked his plume,

Shopkeeper lost his senses,

Cook shed her tears,

So with music, your majesties mourn."

The palace's sadness became the people's sadness, and they, too, began crying. And that is how everyone came to mourn the Hen Sparrow's fate.

As for the Hen Sparrow, she was fine. When she saw her reflection in the water, she thought, "I look pretty in purple." She flittered and fluttered with joy. To this day, Hen Sparrow proudly preens her purple feathers.

Shen and the Magic Brush

China

There was once a boy named Shen. But he was no ordinary boy, for Shen was blessed with extraordinary talent. When he dipped his brush in paint and stroked the color on a surface, his paintings came to life.

One day, Shen heard the sweet chirping of crickets. It made him want to paint a cricket. So he dipped his brush and began painting on the road.

A herald from the Imperial Palace happened to be walking along. "Stop!" he cried, "You are defacing the property of the empress of China!" The man looked down and saw Shen's cricket. Suddenly, the cricket came to life and jumped up.

"I can't believe it!" the man said. "It's magic!" He brought Shen to the Imperial Palace to meet the empress.

The empress looked at Shen and said, "I am very unhappy. My palace is dreary. And I am weary. Paint me something extraordinary to make me happy."

Shen thought for a moment and then bent down. He dipped his brush and painted something extraordinary. When Shen was finished, he picked it up. It was a colorful, ripe peach.

The empress cried, "A peach! You paint me an ordinary peach?! You should be punished!" She ordered Shen to the dungeon and took away his brush.

The empress said, "His brush must contain the magic. Paint me a golden throne!" The herald picked up the brush and began painting but nothing happened. Many tried, but no one could get the brush to work.

Frustrated, the herald threw the brush into the dungeon. Shen was lonely in the dungeon by himself but now he had his brush so he began painting. With every stroke of the brush, he felt better.

Shen painted rolling hills, tall bamboo, a beautiful panda, and a majestic stallion. The walls shimmered with beauty and then came to life. The horse looked at Shen and whinnied.

"Yes," said Shen, "I would like to go home." He climbed upon the horse's back. The empress heard the sound of the horse and ordered the dungeon door opened. Everyone was surprised to see Shen galloping away.

The royal herald and the empress' guards jumped on their horses and chased after Shen. Shen painted a large waterfall, but they passed right through it. Shen then painted a grove of bamboo trees, but they stampeded through it.

Finally, Shen painted a valley behind him. The royal herald and the Imperial guards saw it, but it was too late. Down they fell!

The empress followed too, but on foot. She became lost forever in Shen's elaborate landscape. As for Shen, he returned home to his family. He never once painted for gain. Shen only painted things that made the world more beautiful.

The Singing Turtle

Japan

In the land of the rising sun, there lived two brothers. One was hard-working, and the other was lazy. The hardworking brother cared for his sick mother, fixing her supper even after a long day working in the rice fields.

On the other hand, the lazy brother was never satisfied with anything and always complained. No matter how hard the other brother worked, the family never had any money because the lazy brother spent it all.

One day, the hardworking brother said to his mother, "I am going into town to sell this wood to make us some money. When I return, I will make us supper."

The lazy brother just yawned and lay in bed. Their mother said, "Don't work too hard, son."

The hardworking brother went into town and stayed all day. Unfortunately, he did not sell a single stick. Discouraged, he began traveling back home through the forest. He sat down in front of a tree near a pond where he often ate lunch.

He began to cry. "I have not sold a single stick! My family will have no supper tonight!"

Suddenly, he heard a voice. "Why are you crying?"

The young man looked around and saw no one. The voice spoke again, "Your nose is running. You'd better wipe it."

Surprised, the young man looked around again. "Who is speaking?" he asked.

74

"I am," said the voice. "Look down."

The brother looked down and saw a small turtle. He dried his tears and wiped his nose on his sleeve. "I didn't know turtles could talk!" he said, surprised.

The turtle replied, "Not only can I talk, I can sing too! Anyway, why were you crying?"

The young man told the turtle the whole story. When he was finished, the turtle said, "Since you have fed me so often, it is my turn to feed you."

The brother said, "I don't want to eat you! Besides, I have never fed you before."

The turtle laughed. "No, silly! That's not what I meant. I will sing for you when you bring me into town. People will pay to hear me sing. You can keep the money. It is my gift to you since I have been eating your leftovers and crumbs every time you eat your lunch here."

So the young man agreed and took the turtle into town. The turtle was right. Though the turtle did not sing very well, people dropped many coins in the basket to hear him sing because it was such a strange and wondrous sight to see and hear a turtle singing.

When the young man returned home, he introduced his mother to the turtle and told her the whole story. She said, "You are a fine turtle! Thank you for your kindness!"

The next day, the hardworking brother was bathing the turtle. The lazy brother said, "Give me that turtle. I bet I could bring home more money than you!" He snatched the turtle from his brother and ran into town.

When the townspeople gathered, the lazy brother bragged about how the turtle could sing. The townspeople dropped their coins in the basket and waited for turtle's song. But the turtle wouldn't open his mouth. He refused to sing, remaining silent.

The lazy brother began to yell, "Sing, turtle sing!" But still, the turtle stayed quiet and retreated into his shell.

The townspeople began to yell, "Give us our money back. That's just an ordinary turtle. You tricked us!" They were so angry that they chased him out of town.

Turtle walked home to the family's house. The mother and the hardworking brother were so glad to see the turtle. The turtle told them the story. The mother and hardworking brother invited the turtle to live with them, and he sang happily for the rest of his days. They always had enough to eat, and their lives were filled with laughter and song.

Watermelon

Vietnam

Many moons ago, there lived a great king. The king had a son named An-Tiem. An-Tiem was lazy and often disagreed with his father. This made the king so angry that he banished An-Tiem and his wife to a deserted island, hoping that An-Tiem would learn to become a more productive person.

An-Tiem was allowed to take a small portion of dried food. The dried food lasted one month, and after that, An-Tiem and his wife, Minh, had to forage for their own food.

They lived in a rock cave, and there were no trees or animals on the deserted island. Life was very hard, and they fished at the water's edge or dug for clams in the sand.

One day, An-Tiem found a group of noisy crows descending from the sky. They were fighting over what An-Tiem thought was meat. An-Tiem and his wife hungered for meat so they were determined to take it from the crows.

Gathering stones from the beach, An-Tiem threw them at the crows. Pelted by the stones, the crows were frightened and flew away.

An-Tiem ran to gather the meat, but when he saw the food, he discovered that it was not meat at all. It was some type of fruit. An-Tiem was disappointed, but he brought the strange fruit to his wife.

The fruit had a hard, dark green shell. Peppered with small black seeds, the inside of the fruit was as red as rubies. It was juicy and when An-Tiem and his wife ate the fruit, it melted in their mouths.

76

Minh exclaimed, "Oh, this fruit is delicious! It's as sweet as honey and its juice is as refreshing as water!"

An-Tiem agreed. "This fruit is so good; we shall plant it and cultivate it. From this fruit we can eat and drink. But what shall we call it?"

Minh said, "It is a melon full of water—let's call it watermelon!"

An-Tiem and Minh tilled a large portion of land. They planted the watermelon seeds, and vines grew quickly, producing many more watermelons. Soon, the island had so many watermelons that An-Tiem and his wife could not eat them all.

They left some of the melons for the birds, and when the birds flew in, An-Tiem caught a few and roasted them for dinner. Life was getting easier, but An-Tiem and his wife were lonely.

An-Tiem came up with an idea. "Our watermelons are so delicious that I know other people will want to eat them. Let's carve our names into the hulls and set them afloat. Others will discover the fruit and word will travel to my father that we have discovered a new fruit. The fruit can help bring money to our country, and my father will forgive me."

Minh agreed. "That is a fine idea, husband." They set to work right away and carved their names into many watermelons. They threw them into the sea, and the watermelons traveled far and wide.

Fishermen picked up the fruit and were delighted with the watermelon's sweet taste. They found An-Tiem's island and asked An-Tiem to exchange his watermelons for food, clothes, and money.

In less than a year, many people moved to An-Tiem and Minh's island. They cultivated watermelon and became rich. Word reached An-Tiem's father, the king. When the king heard this news, he was pleased. An-Tiem had proven himself.

It was around the time of the New Year. An-Tiem was forgiven, and he and his wife returned to the palace. They taught the people how to cultivate watermelon. They continued to prosper and live the rest of their days in happiness.

To this day, the people of Vietnam plant watermelons, and this story is told to children. During the New Year's celebration, watermelon is served to honor An-Tiem. Since then, watermelon has been a symbol of forgiveness.

Source Notes

"The Battle Between Wind and Rain" was adapted from "The Battle of the Wind and the Rain" in *Filipino Children's Favorite Stories* retold by Liana Romulo (Singapore: Periplus Editions, 2000).

"The Boy Who Drew Cats" was adapted from "The Boy Who Drew Cats" in *Japanese Fairy Tales* by Lafcadio Hearn (New York: Boni and Liveright, 1918); "The Boy Who Drew Cats" from *Mysterious Tales of Japan* by Rafe Martin (New York: G. P. Putnam's Sons, 1996); and "The Boy Who Drew Cats" in *Tales of Cats* by Pleasant DeSpain (Little Rock, AK: August House Publishers, 2003).

"The Boy Who Wanted a Drum" was adapted from "A Drum" in *Folktales from India: A Selection of Oral Tales from Twenty-two Languages* by A. K. Ramanujan (New York: Pantheon Books, A Division of Random House, 1991) and "A Drum" from Tales of Wonder: India Website: http://darsie.net/talesofwonder/india/drum.html.

"The Cowherd and the Weaving Maiden" was adapted from "The Weaver and the Cowherd" in *Cloud Weavers: Ancient Chinese Legends* (Berkeley, CA: Pacific View Press, 2003); "The Ox Driver and the Weaver" from *Tales from China* by Annie Bergeret and Marie Tenaille (Morristown, NJ: Silver Burdett, 1977); and "The Weaver Fairy and the Buffalo Boy" in *Sky Legends of Vietnam* by Lynette Dyer Vuong (New York: HarperCollins Children's Books, 1993).

"King Crocodile" was adapted from "The King of Crocodiles" in *Malaysian Children's Favourite Stories* by Kay Lyons (Rutland, VT: Tuttle, 2004).

"The Girl Who Used Her Wits" was adapted from "The Young Head of the Family" in *Best-Loved Folktales* selected by Joanna Cole (New York: Bantam Books 1982); "The Youngest, Wisest Wife" in *Around the World in 80 Tales* by Nicola Baxter (Lichester, England: Armadillo Books, 2002); and "The Young Head of the Cheng Family" from *Tales the People Tell in China* by Robert Wyndham (New York: Julian Messner, a Division of Simon & Schuster, 1971).

"The Crab and the Monkey" was adapted from "The Crab and the Monkey" from *Japanese Children's Favorite Stories* edited by Florence Sakade (Rutland, VT: Charles E. Tuttle, 1958); "The Monkey and the Crab" in *Japanese Folktales* by James E. O'Donnell (Caldwell, ID: Caxton Printers, 1958); and "Saru Kani Kassen" from Folk Legends of Japan Website: http://web-Japan.org/kidsweb/folk.html.

"The Hermit and the Worms" was adapted from "The Hermit and the Two Maggots" in *Philippine Myths & Legends* by Gaudencio V. Aquino (Quezon City, Philippines: National Book Store, 1992) and "The Hermit and the Two Worms" in *Filipino Children's Favorite Stories* retold by Liana Romulo (Singapore: Periplus Editions, 2000).

"Lazybones" was adapted from "Mr. Lazybones" in *Best-Loved Folktales* selected by Joanna Cole (New York: Bantam Books 1982).

"The Legend of the Lion City" was adapted from "How Singapore Got Its Name" in *Malay Legends* on the KampungNet Website: http://www.kampungnet.com.sg and "The Singa: How Singapore Was Named" on the Unofficial Singapore Website: Myths and Legends: http://www.geocities.com/TheTropics/5994/singa.html.

"Little One-Inch" was adapted from "Little One-Inch" from *Japanese Children's Favorite Stories* edited by Florence Sakade (Rutland, VT: Charles E. Tuttle, 1958); "Tiny Finger" in *Japanese Folktales* by James E. O'Donnell (Caldwell, ID: Caxton Printers, 1958); and "Issun-boshi" from Folk Legends of Japan Website: http://web-Japan.org/kidsweb/folk.html.

"The Magic Brocade" was adapted from "The Magic Brocade" in *The Young Oxford Book of Folktales* by Kevin Crossley-Holland (Oxford, England: Oxford University Press, 1998) and "The Magic Brocade" in *Best-Loved Folktales of the World* edited by Joanna Cole (New York: Anchor Books, 1982).

"The Magic Paper Charms" was adapted from a Japanese Kamishibai play by Miyoko Matsutani called *The Three Magic Charms* (New York: Twinkle Tales for Kids, 2002) and "Sanmai no Ofuda" from Folk Legends of Japan Website: http://web-Japan.org/kidsweb/folk.html.

"The Magic Pot" was adapted from "Two of Everything" in *The Arbuthnot Anthology of Children's Literature, Third Edition* edited by May Hill Arbuthnot (Glenview, IL: Scott, Foresman, 1961) and *Two of Everything* by Lily Toy Hong (Morton Grove, IL: Albert Whitman, 1993).

"The Magic Teakettle" was adapted from "The Magic Teakettle" in *Japanese Children's Favorite Stories* edited by Florence Sakade (Rutland, VT: Charles E. Tuttle, 1958); "The Magic Kettle" in *Best-Loved Folktales* selected by Joanna Cole (New York: Bantam Books by Doubleday 1982); "The Lucky Teakettle" in *Japanese Tales & Legends* retold by Helen and William McAlpine (Oxford, England: Oxford University Press, 1958); and "Bunbuku Chagama" from Folk Legends of Japan Website: http://web-Japan.org/kidsweb/folk.html.

"The Man in the Moon" was adapted from "The Man in the Moon" in *Flight into Fantasy: A Collection of Vietnamese Tales* translated by Minh Thuy Tran (Maple Grove, MN: Mini-World, 1985) and "The Miraculous Banyan Tree" from *Sky Legends of Vietnam* by Lynette Dyer Vuong (New York: HarperCollins Children's Books, 1993).

"Momotaro, the Peach Boy" was adapted from "Peach Boy" in *Japanese Children's Favorite Stories* edited by Florence Sakade (Rutland, VT: Tuttle Publishing, 1953); a Japanese Kamishibai Play by Miyoko Matsutani called *Momotaro the Peach Boy* (New York: Twinkle Tales for Kids, 1998); "The Peach Boy" in *Japanese Tales & Legends* retold by Helen and William McAlpine (Oxford, England: Oxford University Press, 1958); and "Momotaro" from Folk Legends of Japan Website: http://web-Japan.org/kidsweb/folk.html.

"The Monkey and the Crocodile" was adapted from "The Wise Monkey and the Crocodiles" in *Philippine Legends* by Gaudencio V. Aquino (Manila, Philippines: National Book Store, 1972) and "The Monkey and The Crocodile" in *Favorite Folktales from Around the World* edited by Jane Yolen (New York: Pantheon Books, 1986).

"The Mouse's Wedding" was adapted from a Japanese Kamishibai play called "The Mouse's Wedding" by Seishi Horio (New York: Twinkle Tales for Kids, 1997); *The Mouse Bride* by Joy Crowley (New York: Scholastic, 1995); "The Beautiful Mouse Girl" in *Japanese Folktales* by James E. O'Donnell (Caldwell, ID: Caxton Printers, 1958); and "Nezumi No Yomeiri" from Folk Legends of Japan Website: http://web-Japan.org/kidsweb/folk.html.

"The Noble Frog" was adapted from "The Frog Who Became an Emperor" in *The Peacock Maiden: Folktales from China* (Honolulu, HI: University Press of the Pacific, 2001) and "The Frog Who Became an Emperor" from Professor D. L. Ashliman's Folk and Fairy Tale Website: http://www.pitt.edu/~dash/frog.html#China.

"The Purple Hen Sparrow" was adapted from *HenSparrow Turns Purple* by Jita Wolf (India: Tara, 1998) and "The Death and Burial of Poor Hen-Sparrow" from *Tales of the Punjab* by Flora Annie Steel (London & New York: Macmillan, 1894).

"Shen and the Magic Brush" was adapted from "Sausage Boy and His Magic Brush" in *Silk Tapestry and Other Chinese Folktales* by Patrick Atangan (New York: Nantier Beall Minoustchine, 2004); "Ma Liang and His Magic Brush" in *Tales the People Tell in China* by Robert Wyndham (New York: Julian Messner, a division of Simon & Schuster, 1971); and *Liang and the Magic Paintbrush* by Demi (New York: Henry Holt, 1980).

"The Singing Turtle" was adapted from "The Singing Turtle" in *Kintaro's Adventures and Other Japanese Children's Stories* edited by Florence Sadake (Rutland, VT: Charles E. Tuttle, 1958).

"Watermelon" was adapted was adapted from "Watermelon" in *Flight into Fantasy: A Collection of Vietnamese Tales*, translated by Minh Thuy Tran (Maple Grove, MN: Mini-World, 1985) and "Watermelon" from Bui Van Bao's Illustrated Vietnamese History Series Website: http://kicon.com/stories/watermelon/e_index.html.

Resources

Following are some print and Web resources that will help you to create your own Kamishibai Story Theater.

Bibliography

de Las Casas, Dianne. *Story Fest: Crafting Story Theater Scripts.* Teacher Ideas Press, 2005.

Gillard, Marni. *Story Teller Story Teacher.* Stenhouse Publishers, 1996.

Griffin, Barbara Budge. *Students as Storytellers: The Long and Short of Learning a Story.* Griffin McKay, 1995.

Kinghorn, Harriet R., and Pelton, Mary Helen. *Every Child a Storyteller: A Handbook of Ideas.* Teacher Ideas Press, 1991.

National Storytelling Network. *Tales as Tools.* The National Storytelling Press, 1994.

Say, Allen. *Kamishibai Man.* Houghton Mifflin Company, 2005.

Sima, Judy, and Cordi, Kevin. *Raising Voices: Youth Storytelling Groups and Troupes.* Libraries Unlimited, 2003.

Webliography

The World Wide Web is a great place for story research. Here are some of my favorite sources for Asian folktales and information on Kamishibai.

Ashliman's Folktales and Fairytales: http://www.pitt.edu/~dash/ashliman.html
> Professor D. L. Ashliman, through the University of Pittsburgh, maintains one of the most comprehensive Websites on folk and fairy tales.

Absolutely Whootie Stories to Grow By: http://www.storiestogrowby.com
> A fabulous site with folk and fairy tales from around the world developed especially for kids. Teachers will enjoy the lesson plans and educational content of the site.

Aaron Shepard's Folktales: http://www.aaronshep.com/stories/folk.html

> Children's Author Aaron Shepard offers an extensive collection of folktales, myths, and legends, including stories from Japan and China.

Folk Legends of Japan: http://web-Japan.org/kidsweb/folk.html

> With eighteen illustrated traditional Japanese folktales, this site is a goldmine of Kamishibai stories.

Kamishibai for Kids: http://www.kamishibai.com

> Filled with great information on Kamishibai, this is the site to purchase modern Kamishibai card sets and the Kamishibai stage.

National Clearinghouse for U.S.–Japan Studies: http://www.indiana.edu/~Japan/kamishibai/index.html

> View a Kamishibai story, "The Ogre Who Sank Down to the Bottom of the Sea"; access a Kamishibai teacher study guide; and find a bevy of information on Japan. This site is great for a unit on Japan.

Index

About the Author

Photo Credit: Thom Bennett

DIANNE DE LAS CASAS is a professional storyteller and Teacher Ideas Press author from Louisiana. Now living in Houston, Texas (a Katrina refuge), she continues to tell stories and promote the art of storytelling in libraries and schools.